SYLVIA PLATH: DRAWINGS

SYLVIA PLATH: DRAWINGS

Introduced by
Frieda Hughes

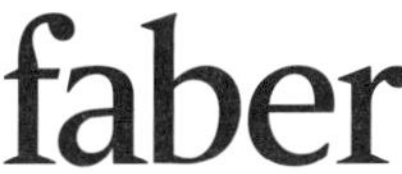

First published in the UK in 2013 by
Faber & Faber Limited
The Bindery,
51 Hatton Garden,
London EC1N 8HN

This paperback edition first published in 2022

Designed by Friederike Huber
Printed in India

A CIP record for this book
is available from the British Library

ISBN 978-0-571-37027-6

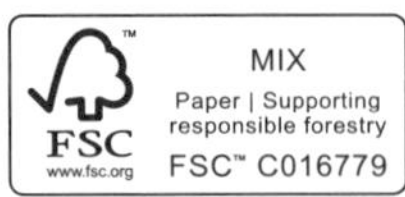

4 6 8 10 9 7 5

Our authorised representative in the EU for product safety is
Easy Access System Europe, Mustamäe tee 50,
10621 Tallinn, Estonia. gpsr.requests@easproject.com

CONTENTS

SYLVIA PLATH AS ARTIST

by Frieda Hughes

MY MOTHER, THE POET SYLVIA PLATH, was born on 27 October 1932 in the Massachusetts Memorial Hospital in Boston in the United States. She lived with energy, passion and a thirst for knowledge, which she directed into her literary and artistic endeavours until her suicide on 11 February 1963.

Although she retained our Devonshire family home after she and my father, the poet Ted Hughes, separated in October 1962, my mother felt the need to be in London. She rented a maisonette at 23 Fitzroy Road, where she lived with my younger brother, Nicholas, and me, for just eight weeks before she died.

Now well known for her semi-autobiographical novel *The Bell Jar*, which was published under the pseudonym Victoria Lucas a few weeks before her death in 1963, it was poetry that first made my mother's name when her collection, *Ariel*, was published to posthumous acclaim in 1965. It was edited by my father using poems from the manuscript that my mother left on her desk at the time of her death.

In 2004, Faber and Faber in the UK and HarperCollins in the US published *Ariel: The Restored Edition*, which used my mother's last actual arrangement of her poems. I very much like having both volumes available, as my father's edition is influenced by his own preferences and what I consider to be his incredibly astute editorial eye, whereas my mother's edition is very much a work in progress, halted in its evolution at the point of her death.

As much as poetry dominated her purpose, however, art was always an important element of my mother's life. As a teenager she was given private art tuition by a Miss Hazelton, and as an adult she wrote in her Yaddo journal (see *The Journals of Sylvia Plath* published by Faber and Faber in 2000) that she had 'dreams of grandeur' in hoping that the *New Yorker* might use her illustrations alongside her written work, as the *Christian Science Monitor* did, 'giving sanction to my running about drawing chairs and baskets'.

Having graduated from Smith College on 6 June 1955, my mother attended Newnham College at Cambridge University from October 1955 to June 1957, reading English on a Fulbright fellowship from the States. While at Cambridge she met and married my father; their wedding took place at 1.30 p.m. on 16 June 1956, by special licence from the Archbishop of Canterbury, in the Church of St George the Martyr, Bloomsbury. They didn't initially make their marriage public knowledge because my mother feared losing her grant.

In June and July 1956 my parents honeymooned first in Paris and Benidorm, before returning to Paris in August, which my mother recorded in some of her sketches. It wasn't until October that year that the couple decided to let Fulbright and Newnham know they were married: fortunately, my mother's fellowship wasn't affected.

In his final collection of poems, *Birthday Letters*, my father mentions my mother's drawings; in his poem 'Your Paris' my mother draws the Paris roofs, a traffic bollard, a bottle, and him too. In his poem 'Drawing' he describes how the very act calmed my mother, and how she became focused and still, and how, as the hours burned away the objects she rendered were tortured into their last position, and the whole scene was imprisoned, for ever.

My mother frequently recorded her literary and artistic evolution in her letters and her diaries; in a letter to my father dated 7 October 1956 (Sunday morning), which is included in this book, she describes sketching cows in Grantchester Meadows only the day before. This was one of several letters my mother wrote to my father from Cambridge during their periods of self-imposed separation, which were intended to maintain the illusion that they were not married.

In a letter to her friend from Smith College, Marty (Marcia) Brown Stern, dated Saturday 15 December 1956, she wrote effusively about her new husband, telling Marty, 'He started me writing & drawing again after a bad winter . . .' She frequently credited my father with inspiring her to creativity when she became stuck or felt herself to have lost direction.

The art of others was also inspiration for her poems; following a request from *ARTnews* in 1958, she wrote poems inspired by the works of her favourite artists. At the time she was teaching freshman English at Smith College, where she had once been a student, and was also auditing an art history course taught by Smith professor Mrs Van der Poel.

On 22 March 1958 in a letter to her mother, my mother was ebullient: 'I've discovered my deepest source of inspiration, which is art: the art of the primitives like Henri Rousseau, Gauguin, Paul Klee, and De Chirico. I have got out piles of wonderful books from the Art Library (suggested by this fine Modern Art Course I'm auditing each week) and am overflowing with ideas and inspirations, as if I've been bottling up a geyser for a year.'

My mother wrote two poems inspired by de Chirico, two by Rousseau and four by Klee. While working on these poems she discussed her influence in an interview on 18 April 1958 that she and my father recorded with Lee Anderson in Springfield, Massachusetts: 'I have a visual imagination. For instance, my inspiration is paintings and not music when I go to some other art form . . . I see these things very clearly.'

Some of my mother's early artwork, together with sketches and drawings over letters and postcards, is to be found with her archive in the Mortimer Rare Book Room at Smith College, Massachusetts, and at the Lilly Library, Indiana University, Bloomington. The pictures in this book, however, are the collection that my father gave to my brother and me before his death on 28 October 1998; they are mostly from 1956, the year of my parents' marriage, and follow my personal arrangement as dates of composition cannot be determined in all cases.

Although my father had divided the drawings between us, my brother asked that I keep them together and look after them until we could, in the fullness of time, organise an exhibition for them. But life got in the way and the years passed, and then, tragically, on 16 March 2009 my brother also committed suicide.

It wasn't until November 2011 that the drawings finally went on show to be sold at the Mayor Gallery, Cork Street, London.

FRIEDA HUGHES, 25 March 2013

DRAWINGS FROM ENGLAND

Sunday morning
October 7, 1956

Dearest love Teddy . . .

A brilliant gray morning . . . sweet gift of an extra hour last night—why can't they do that every day? All the new little girls including Janeen, Dina, Jess, Marie, left for church this morning after breakfast armed with bibles talking about catching the service as if it were a bus. I beamed benevolently at them over my third atheistic cup of coffee and ate my existentialist egg; they really are very sweet, but, my god, so young, so young. In twenty days I shall have completed my 24th year and begun my 25th—I am cruel in putting it this way, but it is true; a quarter of a century gone to pot; and please the lord let there be three more quarter centuries all blessed by your presence, come day, come night, come hurricane and holocaust . . .

O Teddy, how I repent for scoffing in my green and unchastened youth at the legend of Eve's being plucked from Adam's left rib; because the damn story's true; I ache and ache to return to my proper place, which is curled up right there, sheltered and cherished; I am sure you, as a man, will hack out some sort of self-sufficiency in this year, missing only one rib; but I; my whole sense of being is blasted by your absence; and I am again having the most terrible of nightmares, no matter how stoically I go about in the day; it all catches up at night; last night it was you and you—terribly realistic, and then this gruesome series of Ethiopian tribal ceremonies all centering about totems, purifying rituals, and most terrible; perhaps over all was the epigraph of Augustine's I read yesterday—"Verily some have become eunuchs for Thy sake." God, it's terrible; the daily world I can wrest, amid great hurt and void, more and more to my will, but I get to dread the night so; before supper I can feel it coming on me, and I get cloyed at supper and don't want to eat, and rush out into the dark, and walk blindly; and then read, putting off bed and putting it off; and then those damn nightmares.

I will, actually, be glad when classes begin; it will give me a rooted sense of obligation which I need; of speaking with my tutors or dons and on a level in which this howling loss I feel can not yell out; but it gets even and rides me to foam and gnashing of teeth all night.

Yesterday, right after lunch, I took my sketch-paper and strode out to the Grantchester Meadows where I sat in the long green grass amid cow dung and drew two cows; my first cows. They sat obligingly while I drew the first, couchant, its head very cowish, but its body, more like a horsehair sofa, very flat and unmodeled; then, suddenly, they all got hungry and got up in a drove; I think they were bulls; they seemed to have no udders. So I forged ahead, sat down on the river brink, and did a quick sketch of one grazing, or, rather, of several put into one, as they all moved continually, so the side muscles are all wrong, but most decorative; I got a kind of peace from the cows; what curious broody looks they gave me; what marvelous colossal shits and pissings. I shall go back soon; I shall do a volume of cow-drawings.

Various people biking past or strolling to Grantchester stared at me, way out there, drawing the cows; it is so strange, this feeling of abnormality I get away from you— like your experience with police and little girls; I feel, in my singular passions and furies, that I become a gargoyle, and that people will point. One thing, I certainly prefer being alone; I shun people like poison; I simply don't want them; I sit and answer the countless questions of the new girls at table; I find myself being funny and making them laugh with descriptions of people & events, and wonder that I can operate so mechanically, with such little feeling, still retaining the habits of a sane person, without being discovered. There are very dear girls here; sweet, pretty, serious; but I feel like some eon-old matriarch who has been through ice age and 40-day flood; they chirp like new-hatched sparrows. They know I write—the Fulbright commission saw they knew that; I am always rather amazed that, according to Janeen, the commission knows me so well; they must have spied; also, they know I am engaged. Jess endeared herself incredibly to me by asking about what you wrote; "What does your Ted write?" she said. I told her briefly, restraining myself only with great effort from imparting my apocalyptic vision of your blazing, radiant future in which all the Wasters and Spenders of this world stand confounded.

You will perish laughing: I was glancing through the new Varsity handbook last night and discovered a new society on campus: THE CAMBRIDGE MAKERS! O love, guess what, guess founded by whom! Yes, sweet Leftover is providing, hush-hush, the Creative Sounding Board for "secret writers", for those shy undiscovered ones who can get doctored, who I can get their plaints heard; master-surgeons will be invited to speak from time to time; you can be a member through submitting an ms. or (o holy of holies) published work; the impeccable infallible stainless Mr. Levenson will judge whether one shall "sell much of such work". God, how free I feel, leaping such lisping mispronouncings and having direct commerce with the best editors in the world—America, America, God Shed His Grace On Thee.

I brought, from my walk yesterday, a purple thistle and a dandelion cluster home with me, and drew them both in great and loving detail; I also did a rather bad drawing of a teapot and some chestnuts, but will improve with practice; it gives me such a sense of peace to draw; more than prayer, walks, anything. I can close myself completely in the line, lose myself in it; shall I tell you my latest ambition? It is to make a sheaf of detailed stylized small drawings of plants, mail-boxes, little scenes, and send them to the *New Yorker* which is full of these black-and-white things—if I could establish a style, which would be a kind of child-like simplifying of each object into design, peasantish decorative motifs, perhaps I could become one of the little people who draws a rose here, a snowflake there, to stick in the middle of a story to break the continuous mat of print; they print everything from wastebaskets to city-street scenes.

It is as if, by concentrating on the "inscape", as Hopkins says, of leaf and plant and animal, I can know the world a new and special way; and make up my own versions of it. I most do some in London and of Cambridge scenes, and perhaps the NY would take them for their British letters from damn-her-hide Mollie-Panter-Downes. O Panter Panter.

I hate Sundays—no mail. How I miss your written voice —read Sartres' thin simple book on existentialism—That's what I am; damn good little book—please say I can come to London Friday to Sunday & be with you come Carne-Ross or no C-R. My love & more love   Sylvia

A Monday Morning P.S.

Dearest darling Teddy . . . How proud I am How proud I am—the Carne-Ross acceptance seems the loveliest thing yet; I read your letter over breakfast (I have gone into a strange decline over eating—just aren't hungry; the food here doesn't lure me to gorge much, either)—and fought and conquered a huge urge to rudely interrupt Miss Abbott & sweet numberous Co.'S discussion about gowns and bicycle numbers, leap up in the center of the table and shout: MY HUSBAND IS GOING TO READ OVER THE BBC! With appropriate whoopdedos. I AM SO PROUD. I think it will make applying for a teaching job infinitely easier; SO: don't tell them definitely your going to Spain when, but WAIT, cast about for future readings even if you must stay here a month—this is more important to your career (and, probably, finances) than Spain ever thought of being. Ask shyly about your own poems; whatever day you are giving the reading, write ahead and let me come. I refuse to sit here while you are recording Yeats. I have a week of extra nights at the beginning of this term, and I can thus come to London a bit while being able to leave for you wherever you are about Dec. 7. So try to get more readings. I must come every time; if it's not soon, let me come this weekend. The Fulbright can pay for these things; I am—just—beginning to fill my days with proper work; it has taken me a whole stricken week to be able to even read; I don't like this life; but I do it. Like a good girl.

What you wrote about writing stories to one's own strict taste and joy really hit home. I'm doing, really, that; you would be proud, perhaps, a little; every morning I am breakfasted by 8:30, write letters till 9, write and write till noon or one. Then parcel out the day among my howling obligations; met my Director of Studies by accident yesterday and found, to my immense relief that my Chaucer supervisor is obligingly having a baby this term in good Wife-of-Bath fashion, so I won't have her till next, and thus can without panic, Read On. Dr. Krook and Philosophy, (the reading here is beyond belief—must cover all British moralists, plus the literary ones, including Swift and about 15 others!). Such a wise one your little girl will be—it'll give me a rich excuse to buy Books. Thus this term I can get our Big Mss. typed (your fable book, my NY stories, and whatever else you send), draw, and get the writing under a rigid powerful schedule which will take the added Chaucer and German next term without too much of a flinch.

Yesterday I drew a good umbrella and chianti bottle, better chestnuts, bad shoes and beaujolais bottle. Soon I will go about fanatically doing exact and painstaking landscapes of grass-blades—but I bet if I covered a page of grass-blades it would sell; I keep seeing Infinity in a grain of sand.

Read in this terrific Modern Abnormal Psychology book last night (mine) about Schizophrenia—marvelous case-histories, lucidly written; collection of essays by psychiatrists; about manic-depressive geniuses (Beethoven —what do you think of Romain Rolland's "Beethoven the Creator"—referred to; Dickens, Tolstoi & others; also one on hypnotism which I begin today—excellent bibliographies). Finished a rather good 8-page NY story about the dreamless woman yesterday; strange how competent I get to feel with each new story, even if the story, as such, mightn't sell—I begin "The Invisible Man" today—write o write when I can come to London—for two days??—with love, your admiring SYLVIA

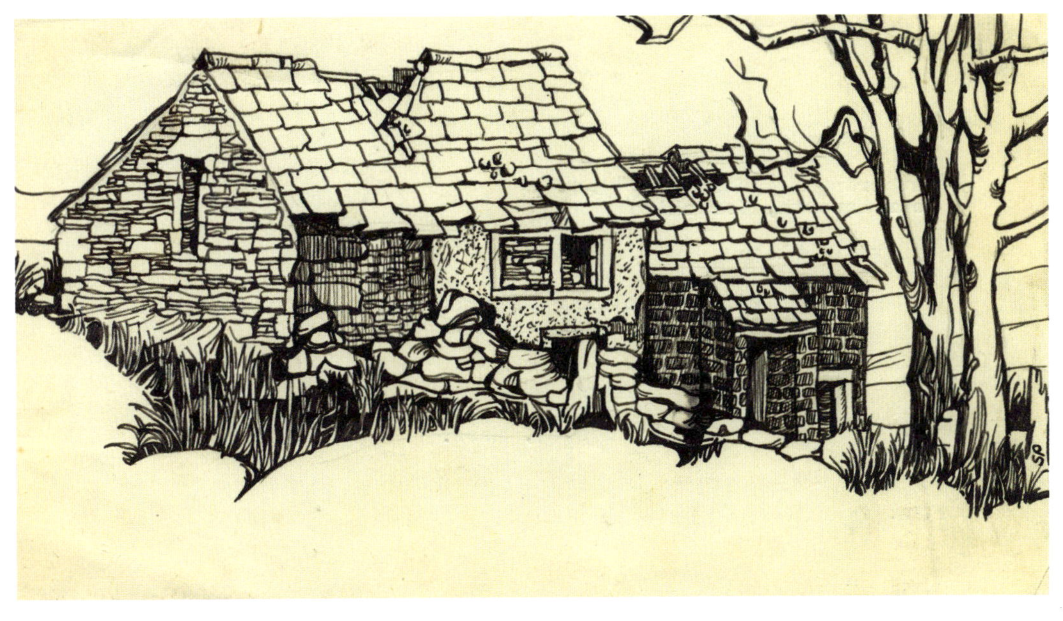

Wuthering Heights Today, 1956, near Haworth, Yorkshire
Pen and ink on paper, signed with initials, typed with title, 11.2 x 19.8cm

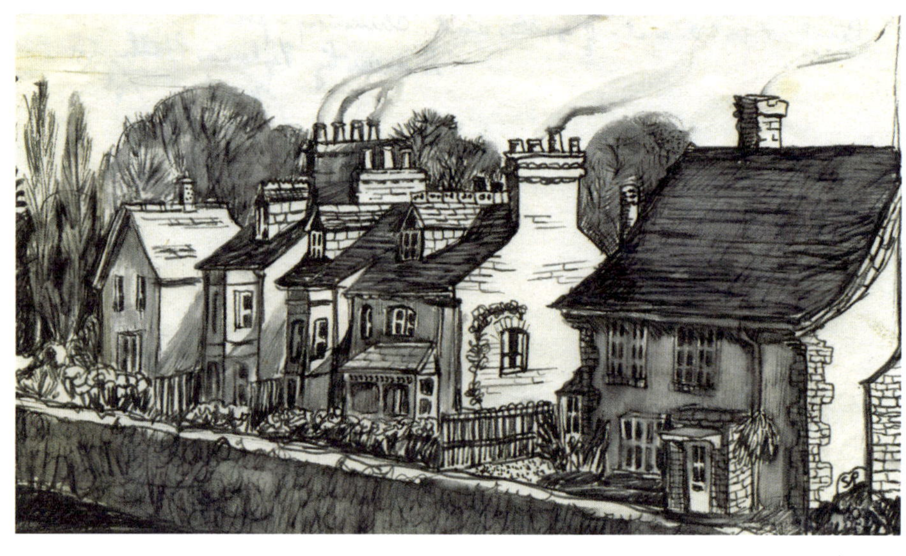

Cambridge: a View of Gables and Chimney-pots, c. 1955
Ink and wash on paper, signed with initials lower right, 10 x 16.8cm
(framed with Brasilia, right)

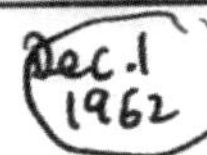

Original carbon of Brasilia typed by Plath, Devon 1962
(Framed with *Cambridge: a View of Gables and Chimney-pots*, left)

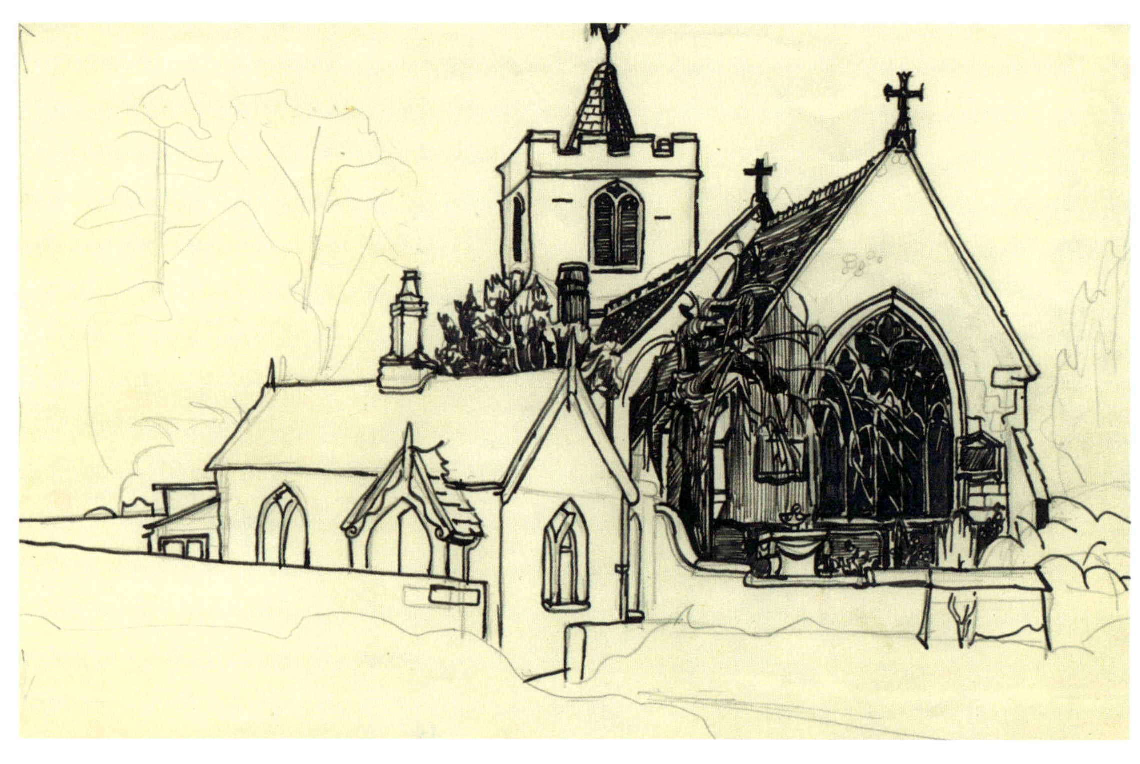

Study of a Church and Chapel, 1956
Pencil, pen and ink on paper, 14 x 21cm

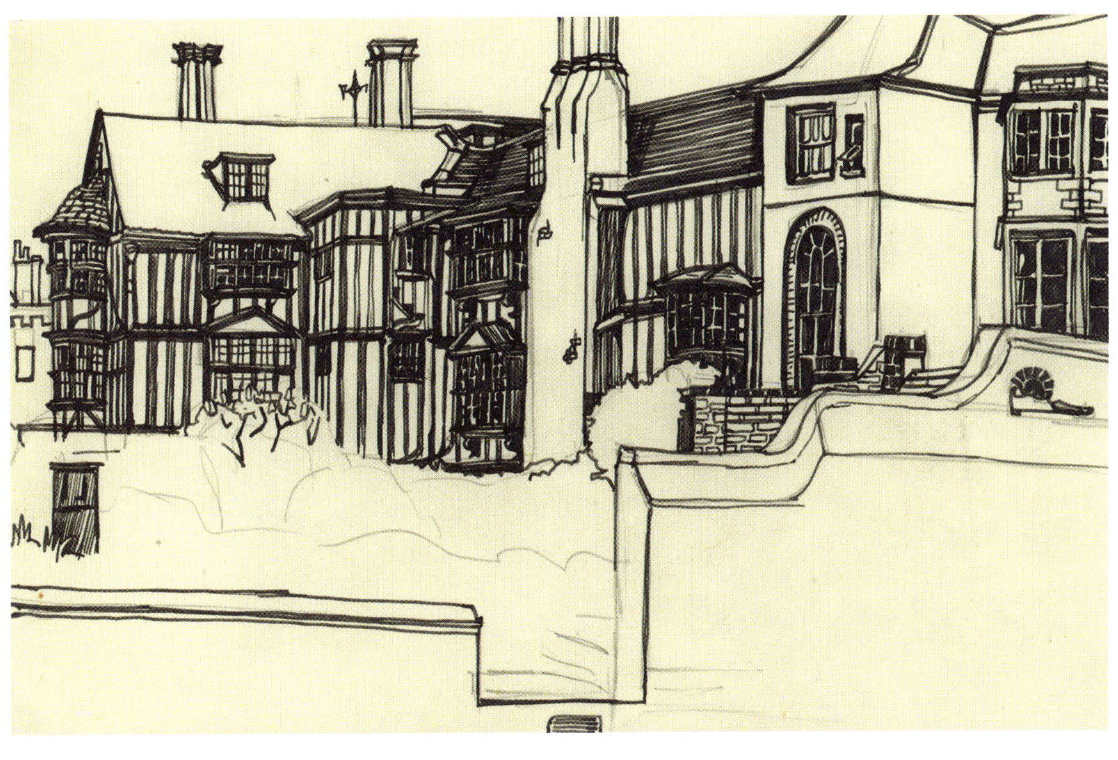

Study of a Manor, 1956
Pencil, pen and ink on paper, 14 x 21.5cm

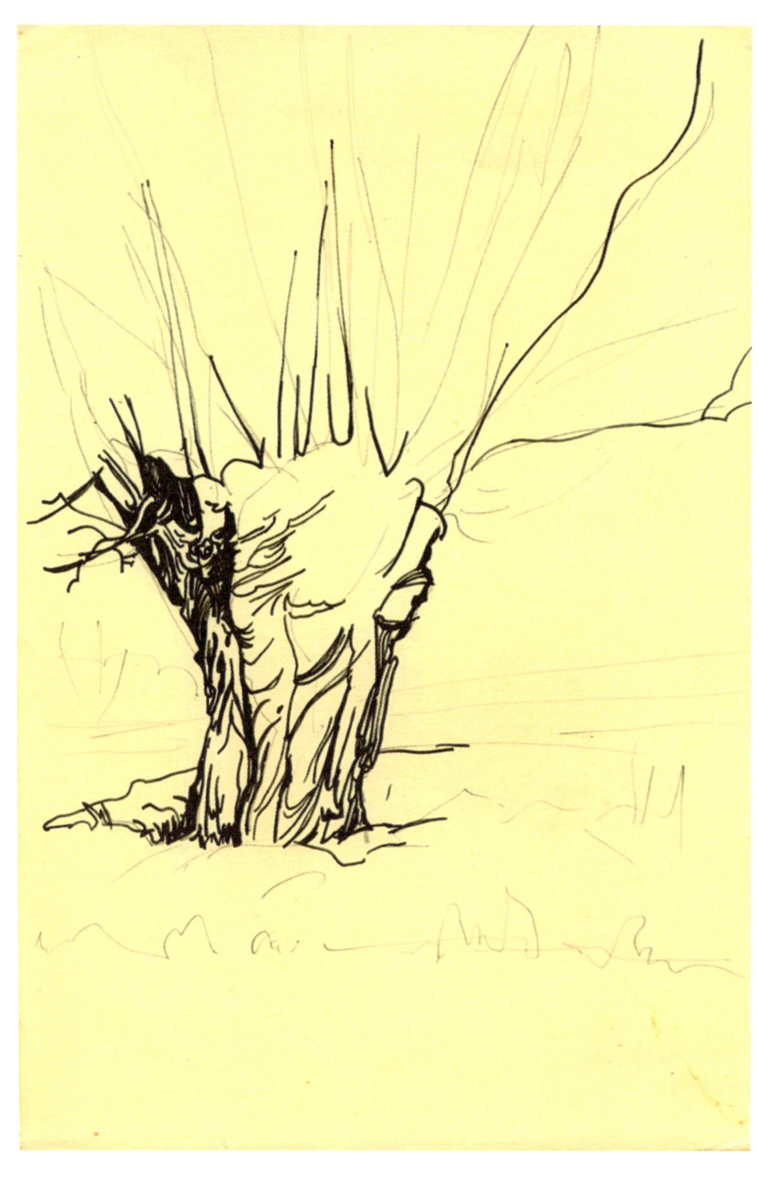

Willow near Grantchester
Pencil, pen and ink on paper, 21.5 x 14cm

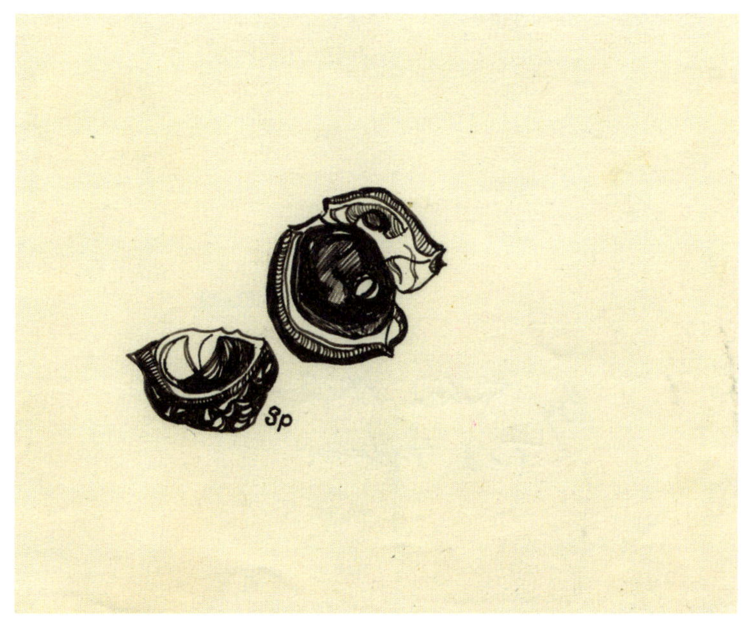

Horse Chestnut, 1956
Pen and ink on paper, 11.8 x 14cm

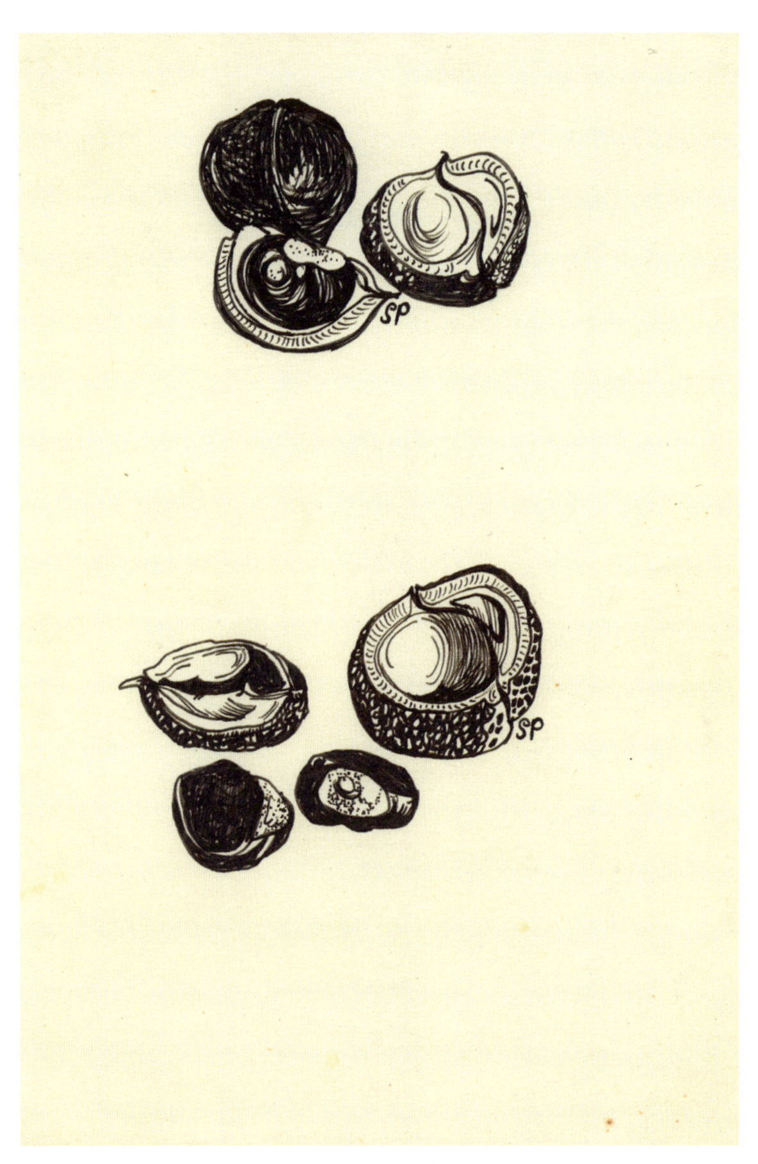

Horse Chestnuts, 1956
Pen and ink, 21.5 x 14cm

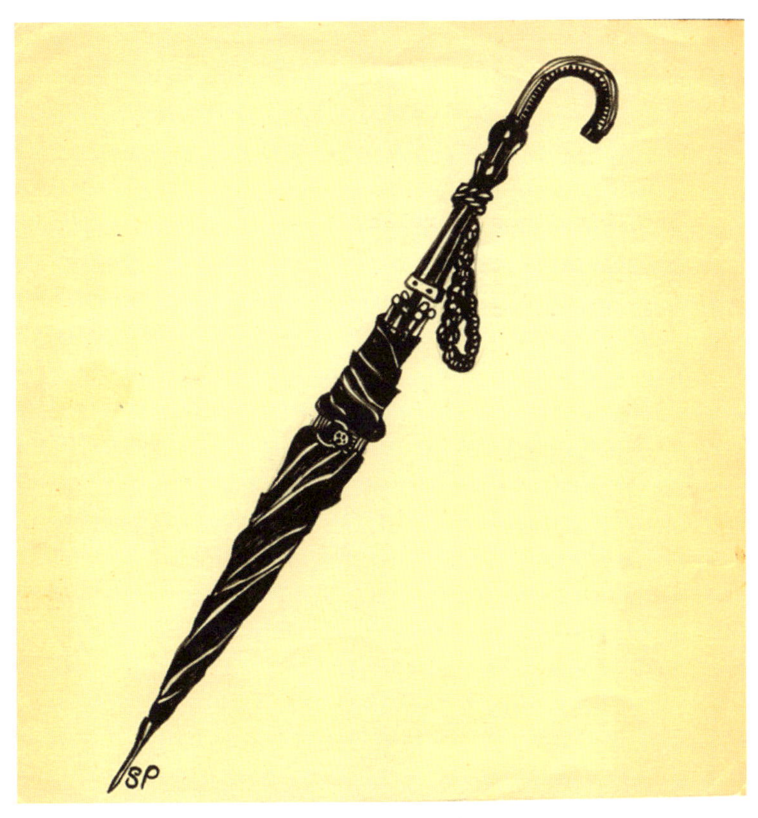

The Ubiquitous Umbrella, 1955–56
Pen and ink on paper, 15 x 14cm

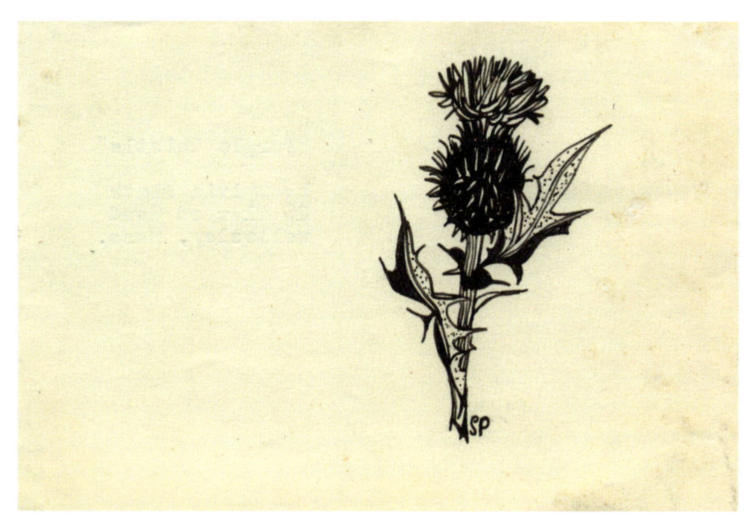

Purple Thistle, 1956
Pen and ink on paper, 9.5 x 13.8cm

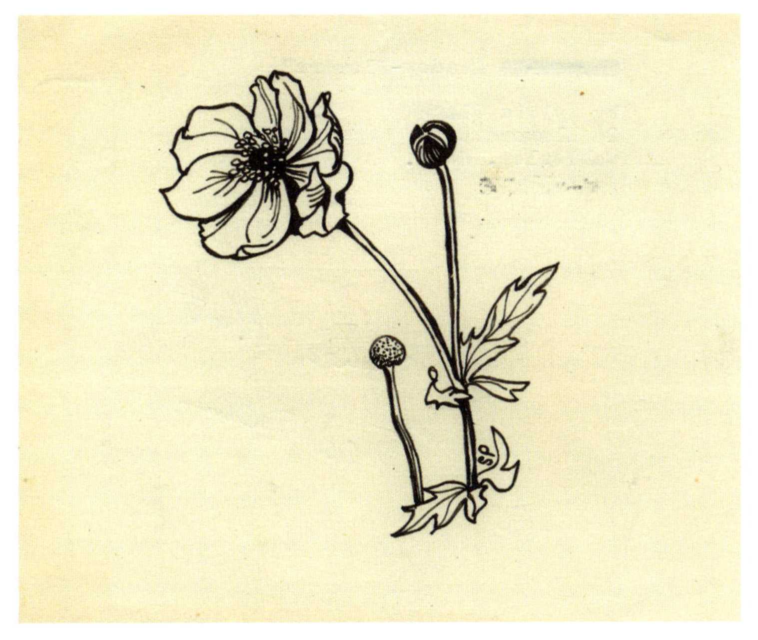

Meadow-Flowers
Pen and ink on paper, 12 x 14cm

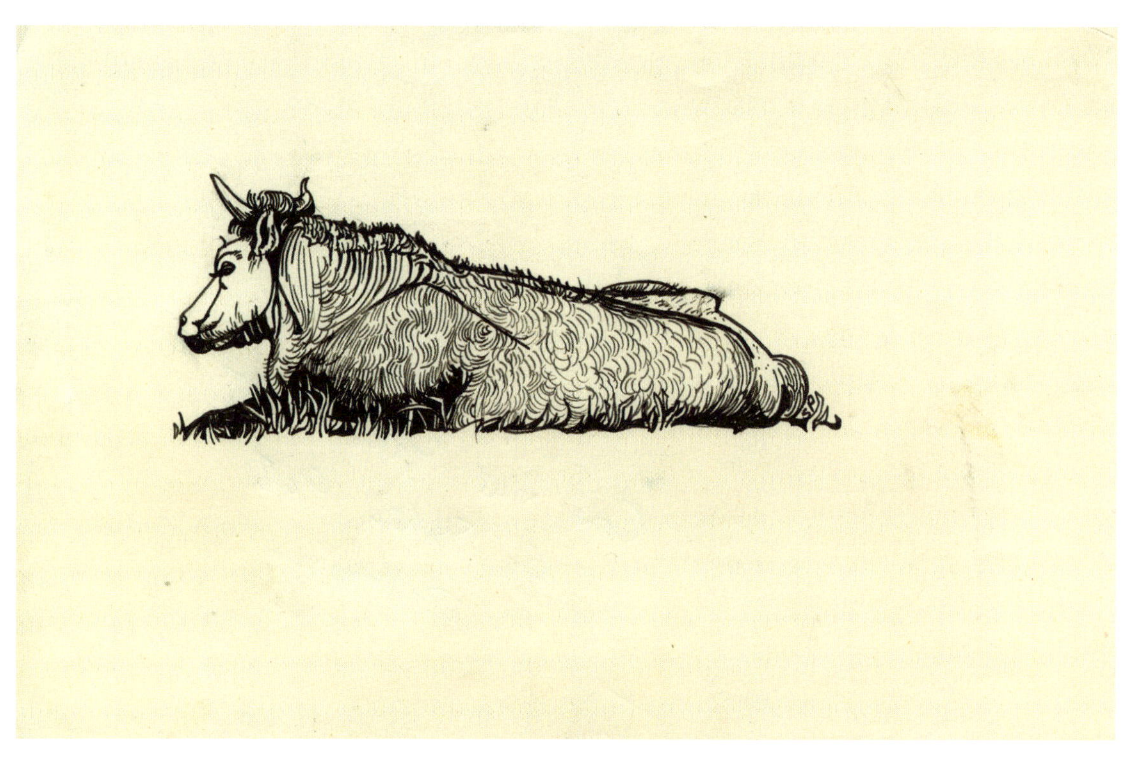

Bull near Grantchester, 1956
Pen and ink on paper, 14 x 21.5cm

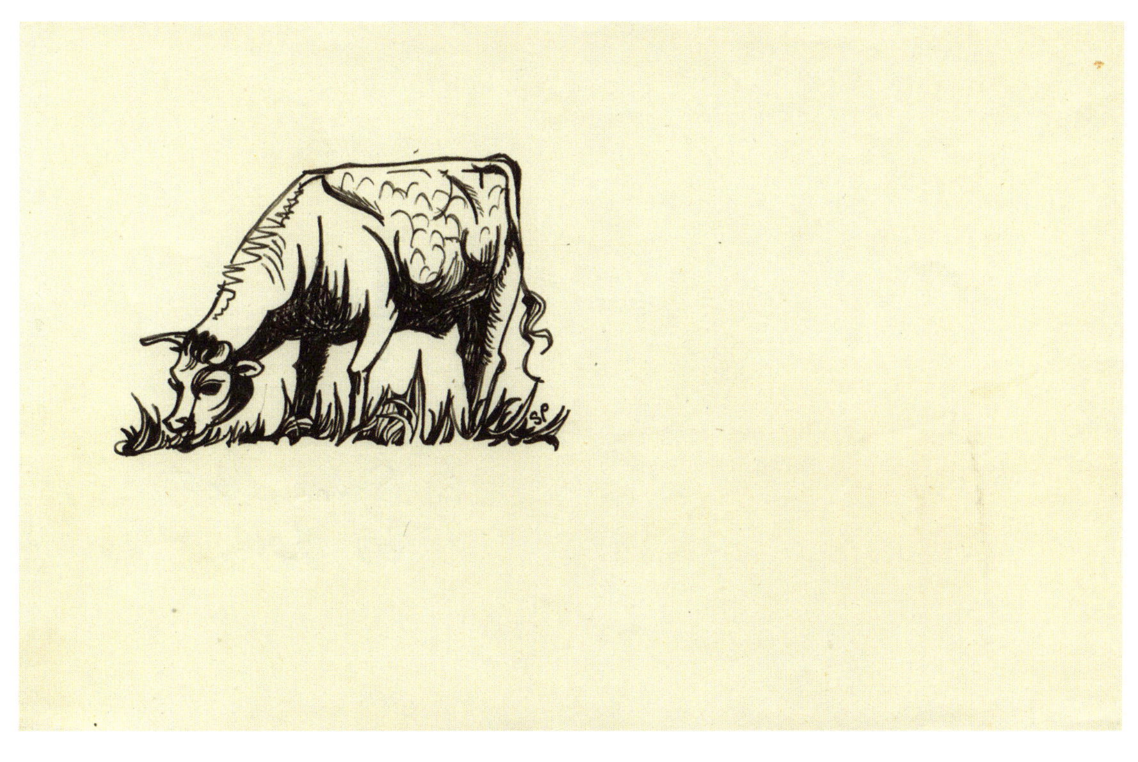

Bull, 1956
Pen and ink on paper, 14 x 21.5cm

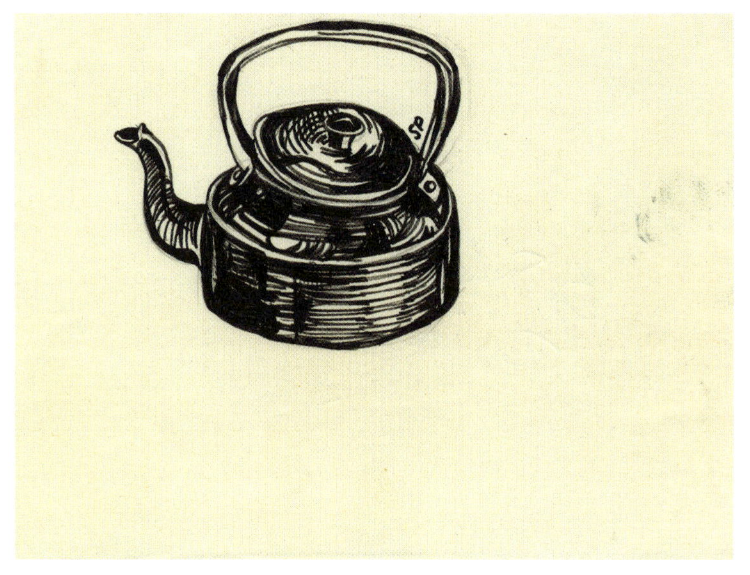

Kettle, 1956
Pen and ink on paper, 11 x 14cm

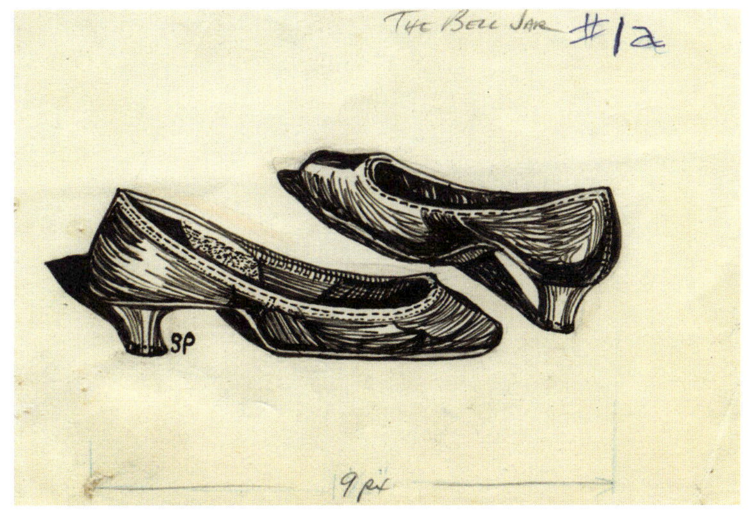

Study of Shoes, 1956
Pen and ink on paper, 10 x 14cm
(intended for use in *The Bell Jar*, 1963)

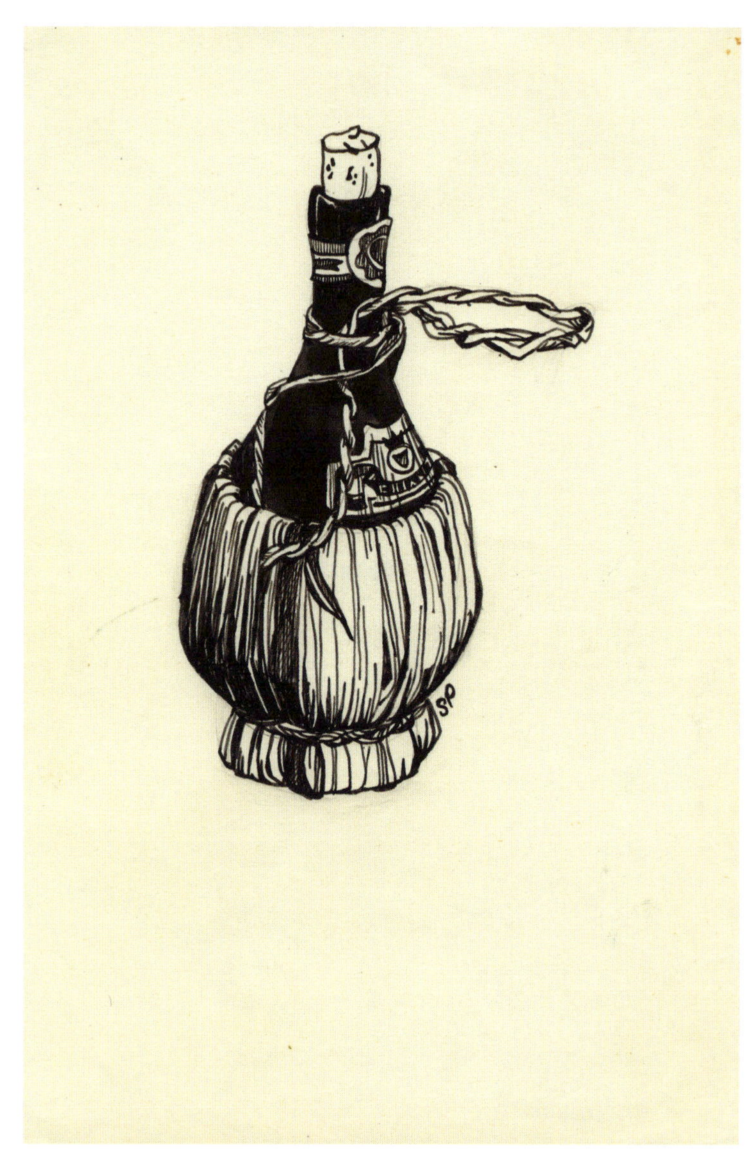

Chianti Bottle
Pen and ink on paper, 21.5 x 14cm

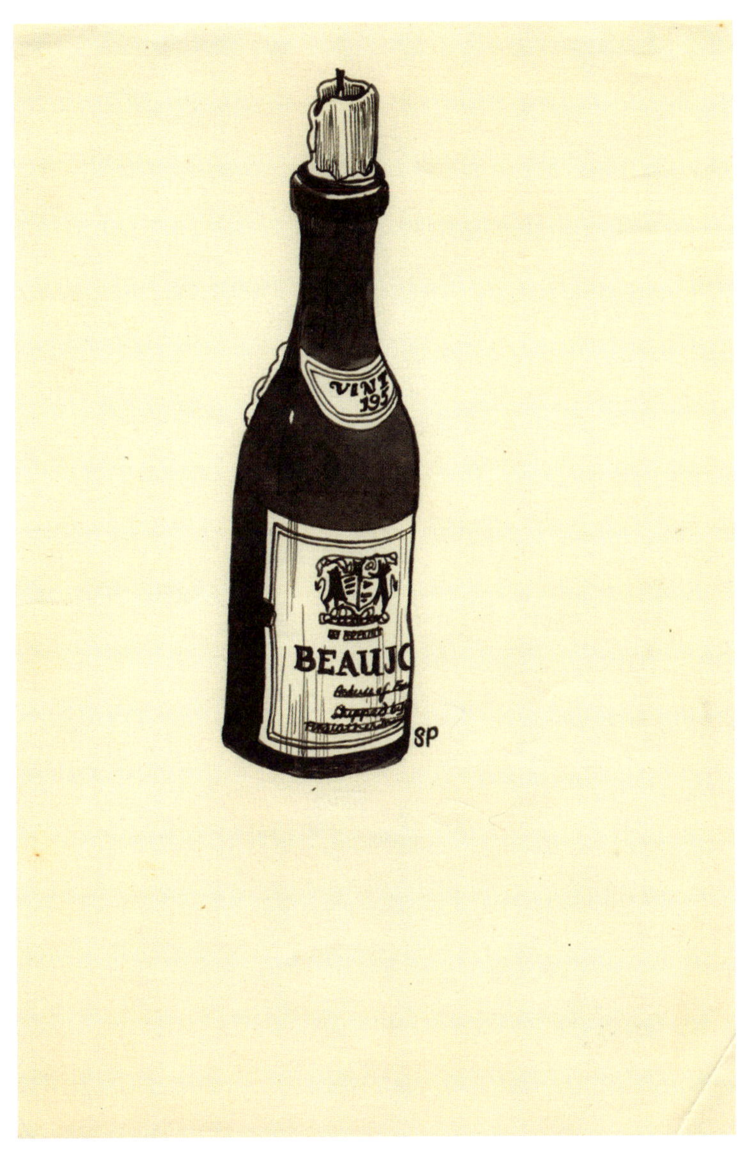

Beaujolais Bottle, 1956
Pen and ink on paper, 21.5 x 14cm

DRAWINGS FROM FRANCE

Hotel Des Deux Continents
Paris, France
August 25, 1956

Dearest of Mothers,

It is now Saturday the 25th and Warren is sitting on our bed reading your letter while Ted is at the bowl scrubbing the last dirt out of his shirt, which only his hands are strong enough to get clean. Our trip up was really wearying, but much of it fun. I enjoyed the last week in Benidorm more than any yet, as if I were just coming awake to the town and went about with Ted doing detailed pen-and-ink sketches while he sat at my side and read, wrote, or just meditated. He loves to go with me while I sketch and is very pleased with my drawings and sudden return to sketching. Wait till you see these few of Benidorm—the best I've ever done in my life, very heavy stylized shading and lines; very difficult subjects, too: the peasant market (the peasants crowded around like curious children, and one little man who wanted me to get his stand in, too, hung a wreath of garlic over it artistically so I would draw that); a composition of three sardine boats on the bay with their elaborate lights, and a good one of the cliff-headland with the houses over the sea. I'm going to write an article for them and send them to the *Monitor*. I feel I'm developing a kind of primitive style of my own which I am very fond of. Wait till you see. The Cambridge sketch was nothing compared to these. Ted wants me to do more and more. . . .

The trip to Paris was exhausting, leaving at three in the afternoon and getting in at nine the next morning. We were stiff and cramped, but revived over breakfast on the train and had a delightful, gray morning sitting by the Seine, watching the fishermen on the bank and the women on the barges hanging out washing. Such a joy to have subtle, gray weather after the blank blazing sun. Life is so much heightened by contrasts. I am actually looking extremely forward to going up to Ted's wuthering-heights home next week. For all my love of the blazing sun, there is a lack of intellectual stimulus in countries as hot as Spain.

Warren arrived early yesterday morning, and we fed him breakfast and made him take a nap all afternoon. . . .

. . . Paris is not *French* Paris; the only language you hear is English, and I am glad that Ted and I can give Warren the atmosphere as we know it, not as the tourists find it. Hope we can live here a year some day (but not in July and August), because of the continuous fine movies, plays, and art exhibits. I really love this city above any I've ever been in; it is dear and graceful and elegant and what one makes it. I could never live in London or New York or Madrid, or even Rome, but here, yes. . . .

Hope your trip back was not full of mal de mer; rest before school. We all love you dearly . . .

Sivvy

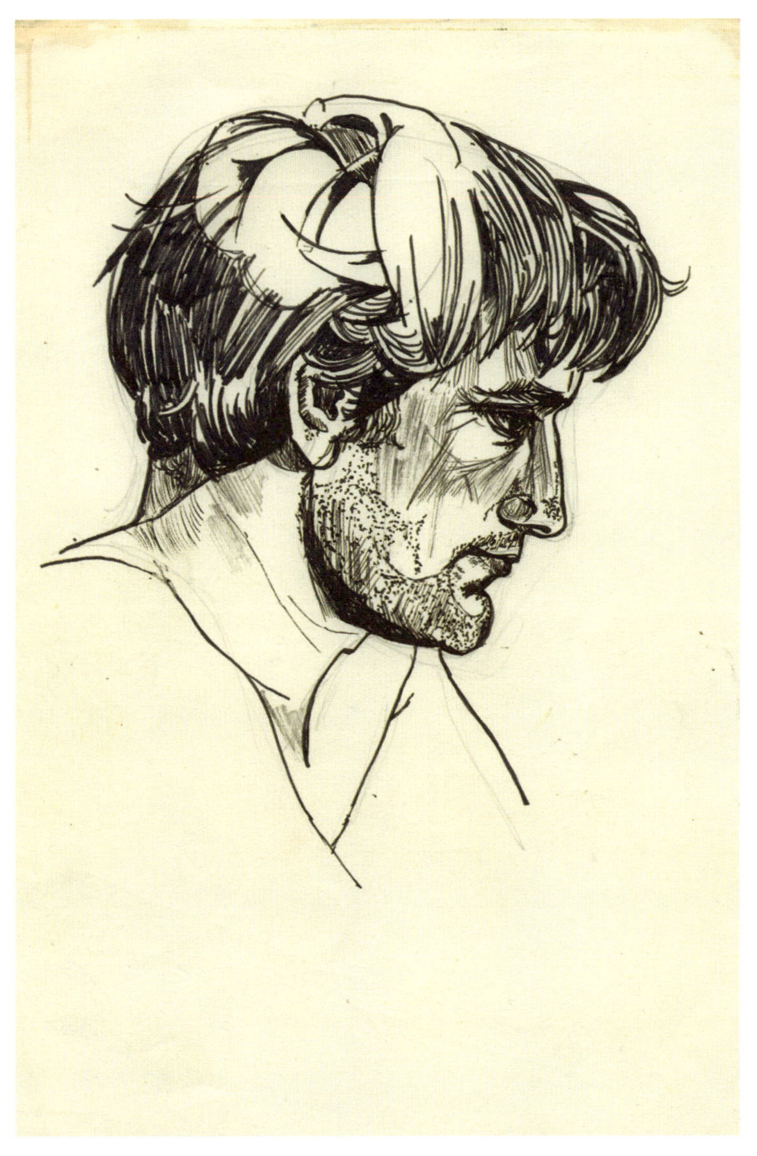

Ted Hughes, 1956
Pen and ink on paper, 21.5 x 14cm

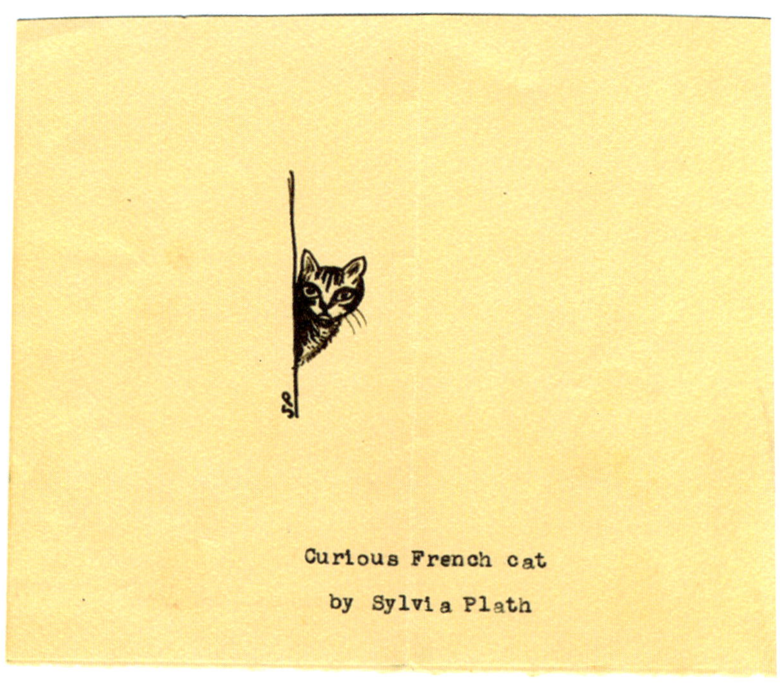

Curious French Cat, 1956
Pen and ink on paper, 12.6 x 15.3cm

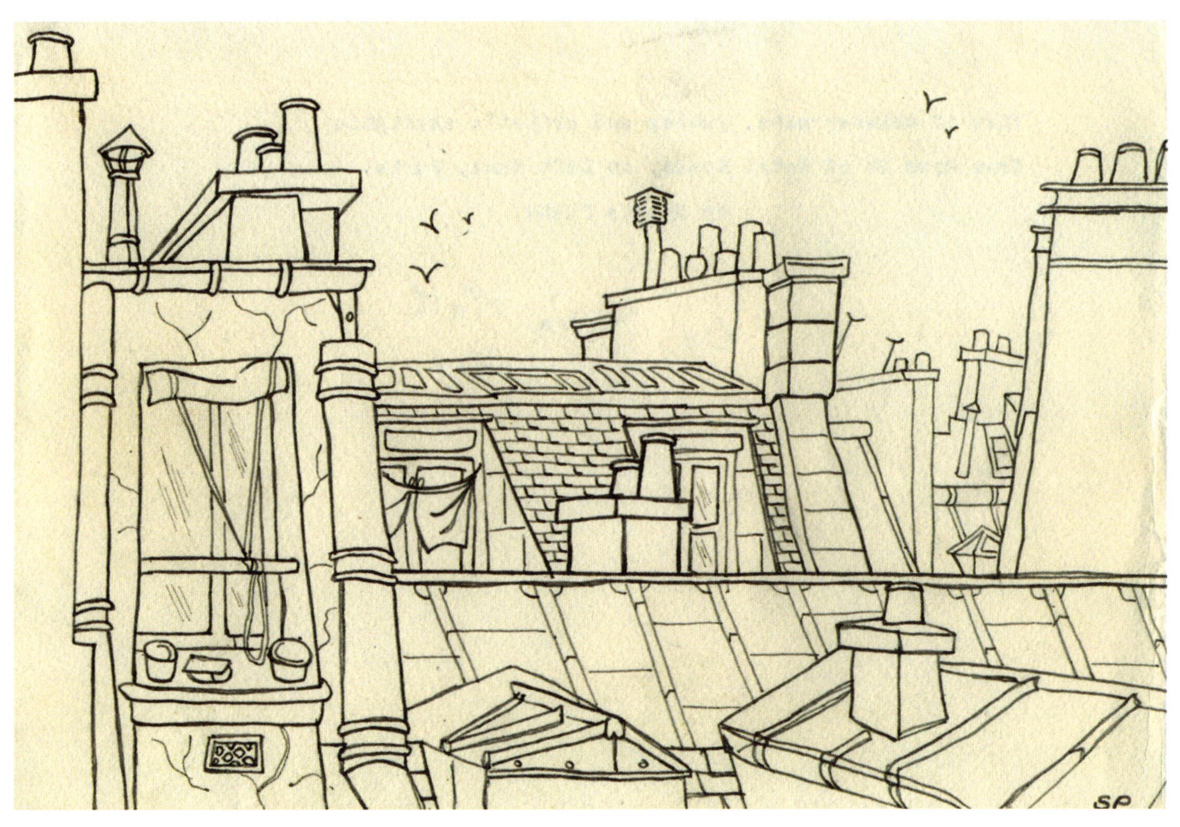

View of Chimney-Pots, Gables and Artist's Skylights from Room 26 of Hotel Bearn
on Left Bank, Paris, 1956
Pen and ink on paper, 15.2 x 22cm

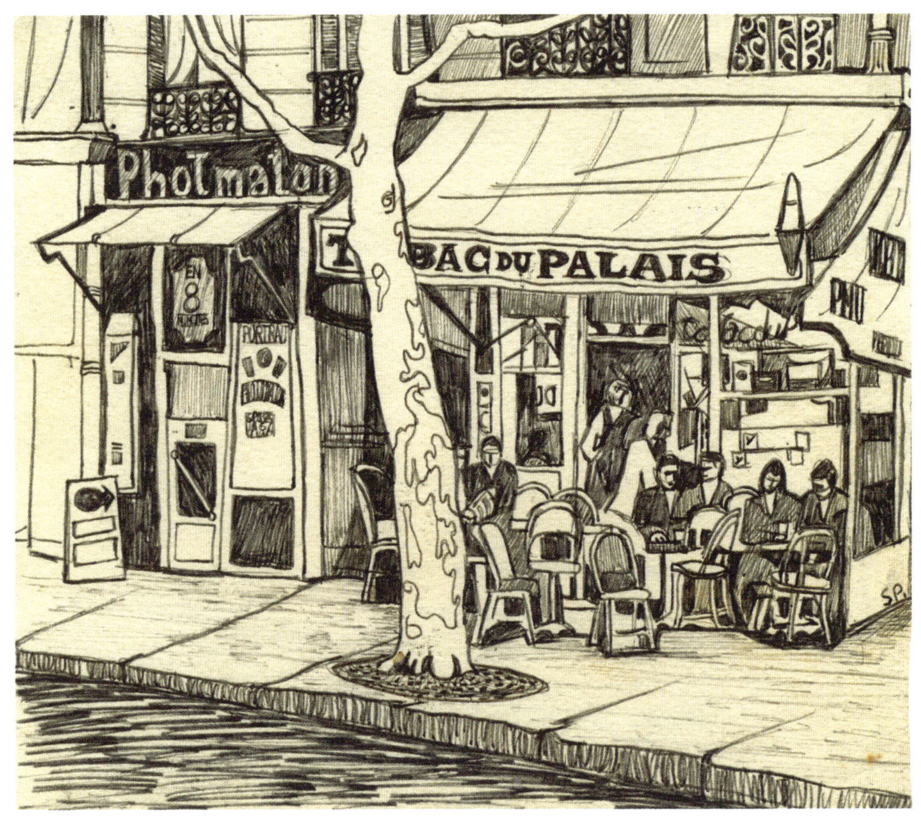

Tabac Opposite Palais de Justice, 1956
Pen and ink on paper, 15.2 x 17cm

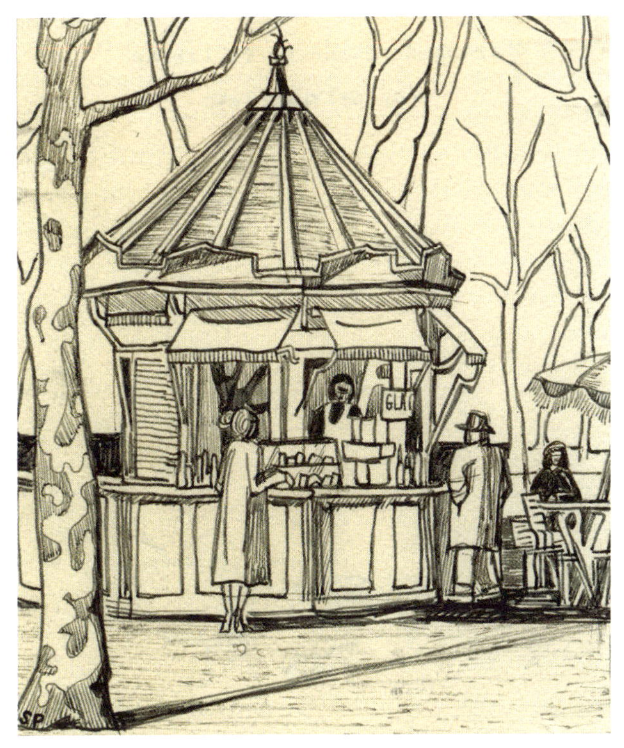

Citronnade Stand in Tuileries, 1956
Pen and ink on paper, 14 x 11.5cm

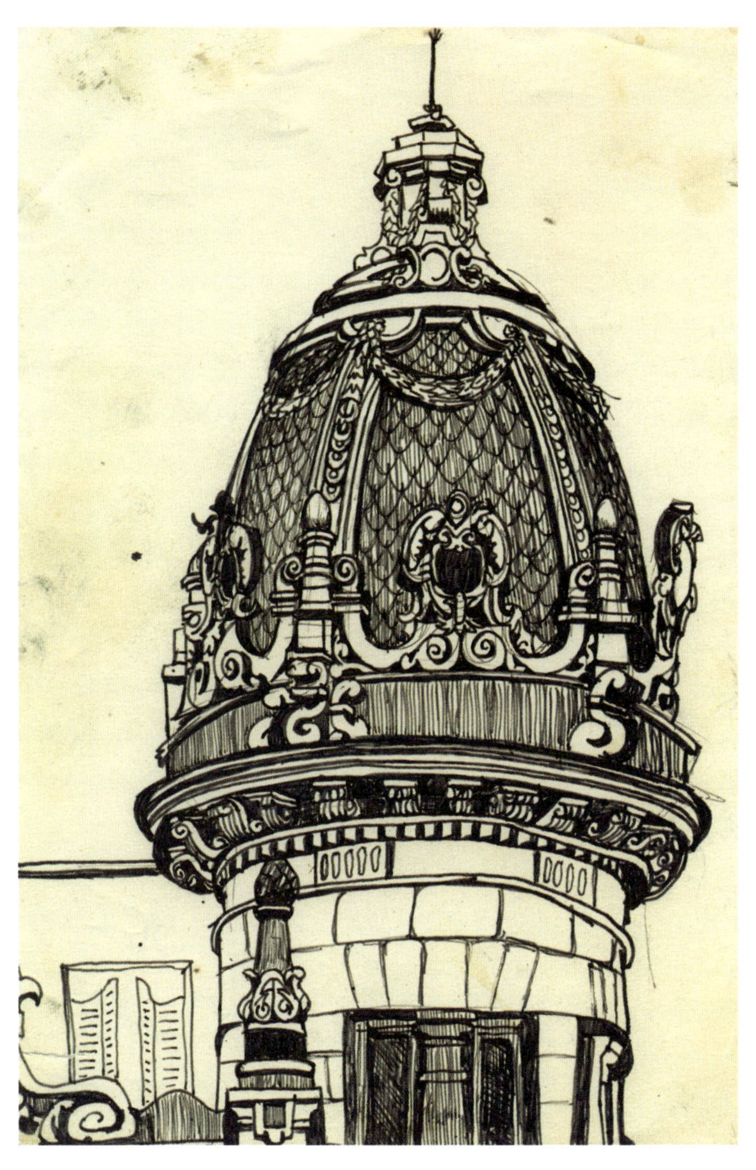

Paris Rooftops, 1956
Pen and ink on paper, 21.5 x 14cm

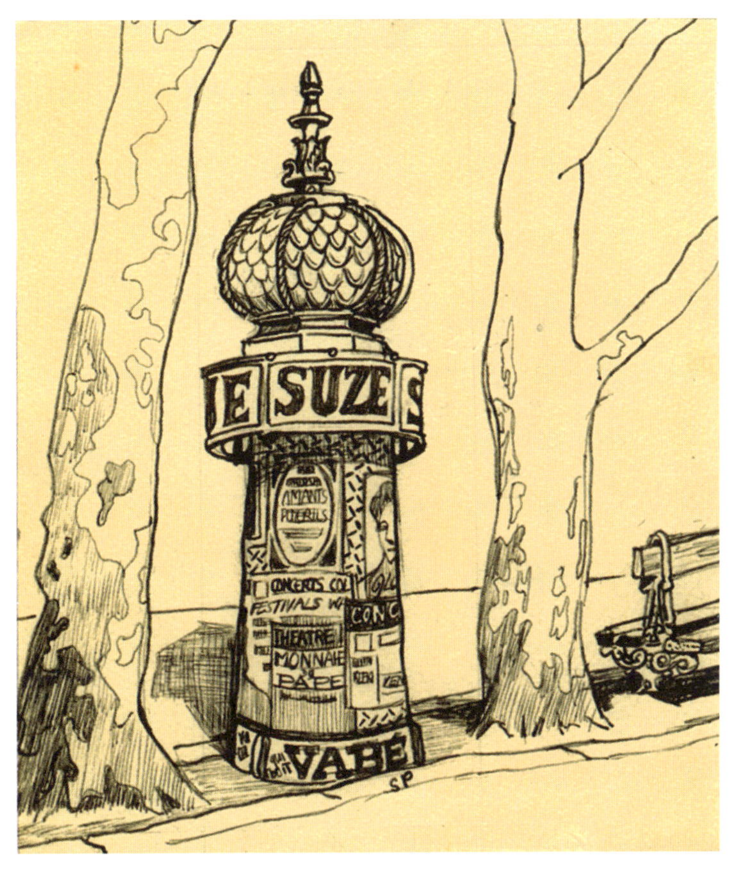

Colourful Kiosque near Louvre, 1956
Pen and ink on paper, 16 x 13cm

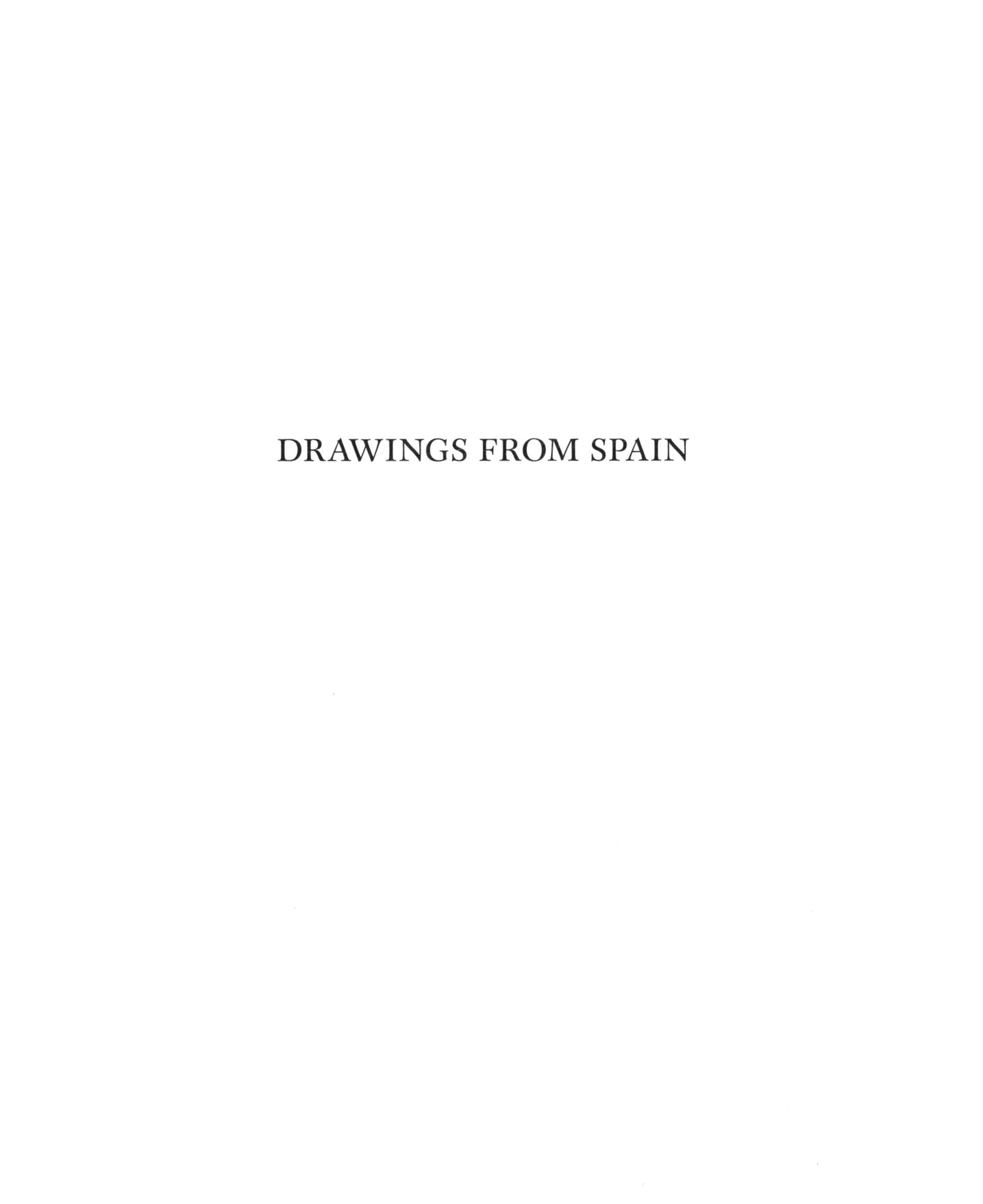

DRAWINGS FROM SPAIN

October 23, 1956

Dearest Mother,

This will be an installment letter, coming so soon after the last. It is chiefly to tell you another bit of good news . . . I got a beautiful check for over £9 this morning (that's about $26) from guess who! THE CHRISTIAN SCIENCE MONITOR!!

At their pay-rates, this seems like a rather glorious sum. You will be awe-struck, I think, when you see what they bought: a short little article on Benidorm (that lovely little Spanish town where we spent five weeks on our honeymoon) and four of the best sketches in pen-and-ink I've ever done. I think that these drawings will also amaze you. It shows what I've done since going out with Ted. Every drawing has in my mind and heart a beautiful association of our sitting together in the hot sun, Ted reading, writing poems, or just talking with me. Please get lots and lots of copies of each article. The sketches are very important to me. The one of the sardine boats is the most difficult and unusual I've ever done. . . . The castle rock and houses for design is a favorite; the stairway is my least favorite, but not too bad. I hope you love them; send them to Mrs. Prouty, please; show her how creative Ted's made me! . . .

. . . When Ted and I begin living together we shall become a team better than Mr. and Mrs. Yeats—he being a competent astrologist, reading horoscopes, and me being a tarot-pack reader, and, when we have enough money, a crystal-gazer. Will let you know of our decision after this weekend . . . It is ridiculous for us to separate our forces when it is such a magnificently "aspected" year—I'm typing a book of his poems (an impressive 50 pages) for a contest at the end of November . . . I'd love Cambridge so if he were here. There's no question of his supporting me, either, since all he'll earn will have to go for ship fare to America. I write and think and study perfectly when with him; apart, I'm split and only can work properly in brief, stoic spells. . . .

Later: WELL, HERE IS THE LATEST BULLETIN: Ted came up from London tonight . . .

Both of us have been literally sick to death being apart, wasting all our time and force trying to cope with the huge, fierce sense of absence. SO: Spain is out. Ted is coming to live and work in Cambridge for the rest of the year. In the next two weeks we are going on a rigorous campaign of making our marriage public; first, to my philosophy supervisor; next, to the Fulbright; next, Newnham. We are married and it is impossible for either of us to be whole or healthy apart. . . . I can write and do good exams if my Teddy is with me. Do write and stand by. We will be so happy together from December 7 on. Wish us luck with the authorities.

Your own loving Sivvy

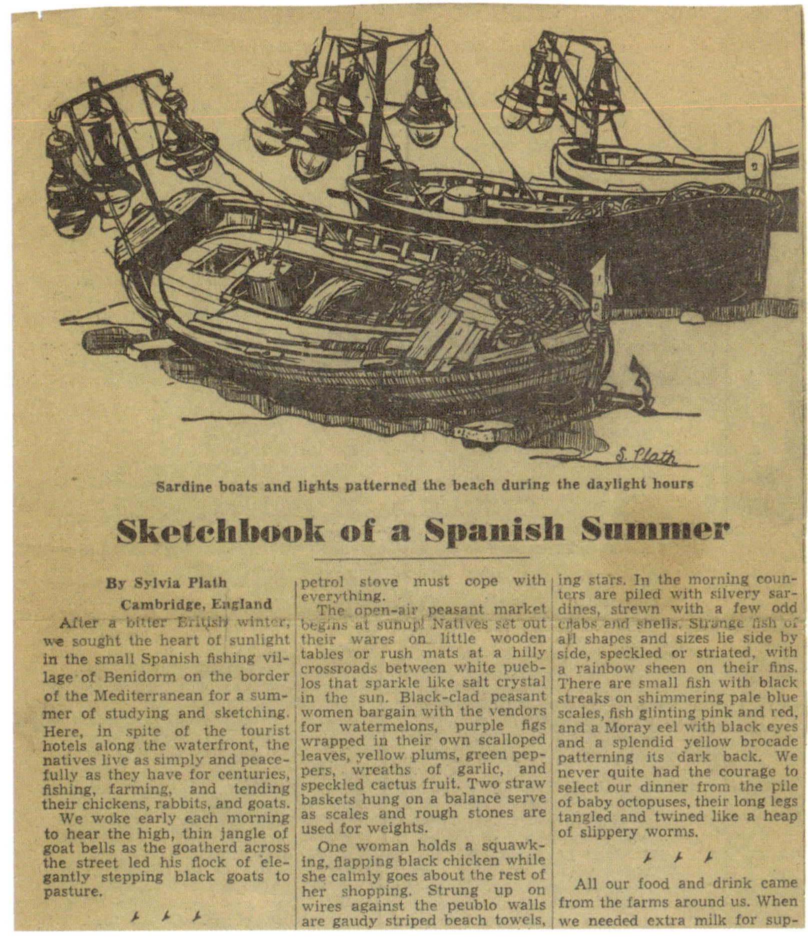

Sardine boats and lights patterned the beach during the daylight hours

Sketchbook of a Spanish Summer

By Sylvia Plath

Cambridge, England

After a bitter British winter, we sought the heart of sunlight in the small Spanish fishing village of Benidorm on the border of the Mediterranean for a summer of studying and sketching. Here, in spite of the tourist hotels along the waterfront, the natives live as simply and peacefully as they have for centuries, fishing, farming, and tending their chickens, rabbits, and goats.

We woke early each morning to hear the high, thin jangle of goat bells as the goatherd across the street led his flock of elegantly stepping black goats to pasture.

petrol stove must cope with everything.

The open-air peasant market begins at sunup. Natives set out their wares on little wooden tables or rush mats at a hilly crossroads between white pueblos that sparkle like salt crystal in the sun. Black-clad peasant women bargain with the vendors for watermelons, purple figs wrapped in their own scalloped leaves, yellow plums, green peppers, wreaths of garlic, and speckled cactus fruit. Two straw baskets hung on a balance serve as scales and rough stones are used for weights.

One woman holds a squawking, flapping black chicken while she calmly goes about the rest of her shopping. Strung up on wires against the peublo walls are gaudy striped beach towels,

ing stars. In the morning counters are piled with silvery sardines, strewn with a few odd crabs and shells. Strange fish of all shapes and sizes lie side by side, speckled or striated, with a rainbow sheen on their fins. There are small fish with black streaks on shimmering pale blue scales, fish glinting pink and red, and a Moray eel with black eyes and a splendid yellow brocade patterning its dark back. We never quite had the courage to select our dinner from the pile of baby octopuses, their long legs tangled and twined like a heap of slippery worms.

All our food and drink came from the farms around us. When we needed extra milk for sup-

Detail from 'Sketchbook of a Spanish Summer', *Christian Science Monitor*,
5 November, 1956

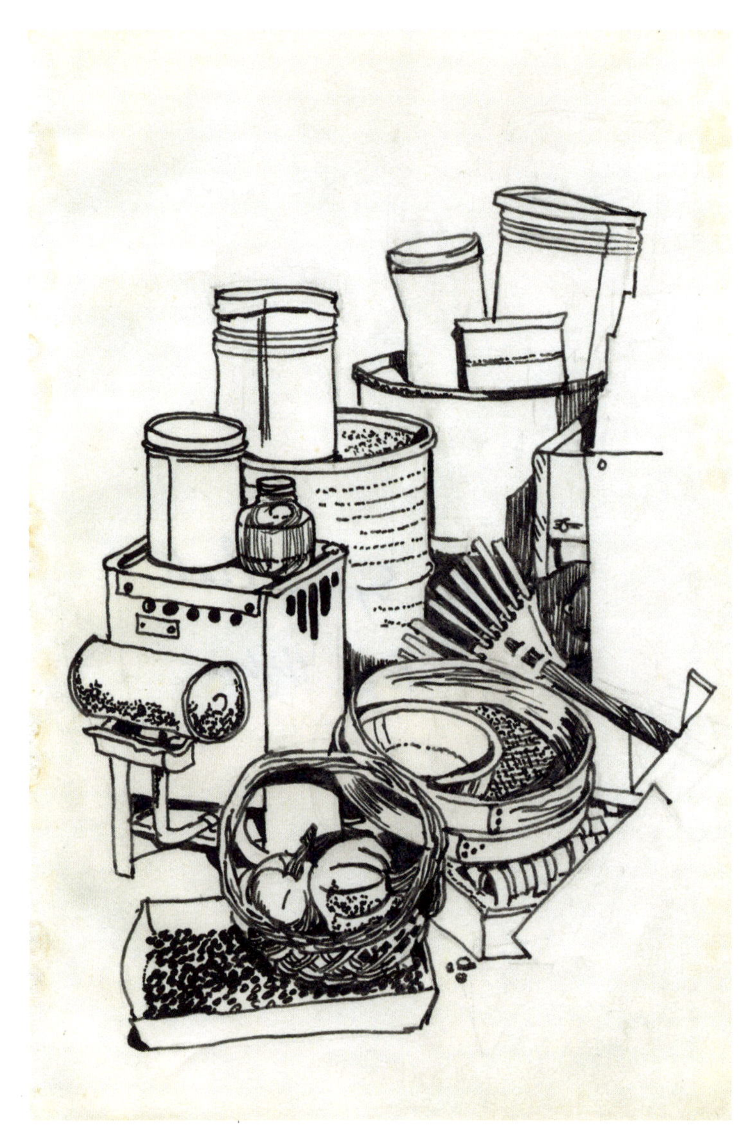

Still Life with Pots and Fruits, 1956
Pen and ink on paper, 21 x 13cm

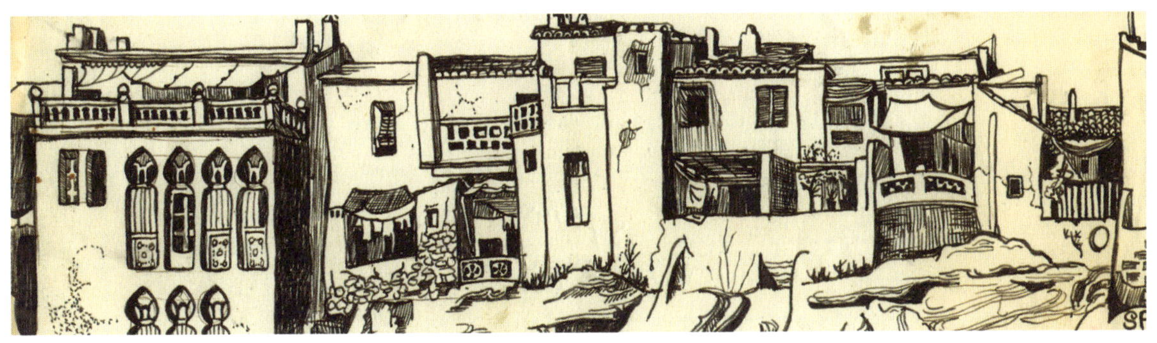

White Plaster Tenements on Cliffs over Fishing Bay, 1956
Pen and ink on paper, 6.4 x 21.5cm

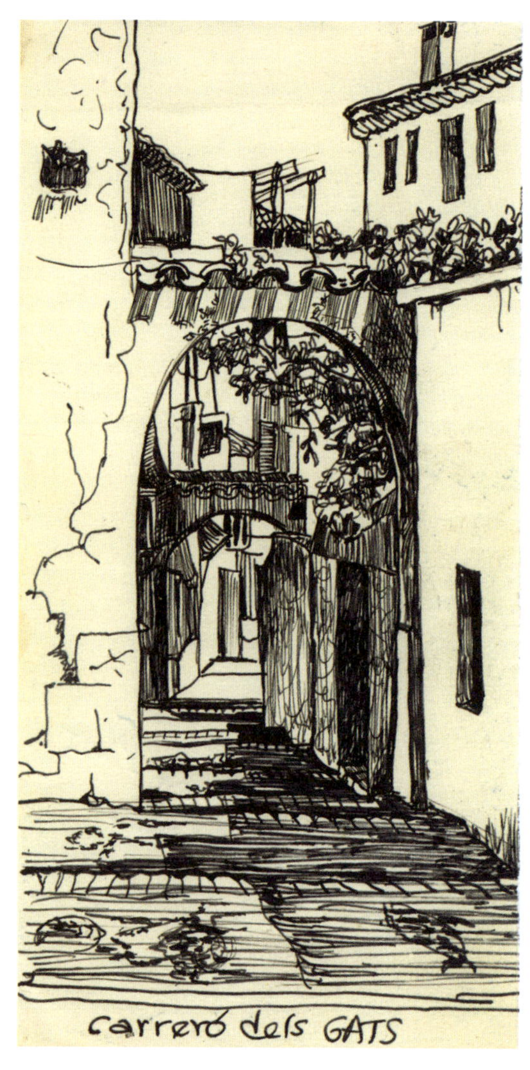

Carreró dels Gats, 1956
Pen and ink on paper, 19.8 x 9.5cm

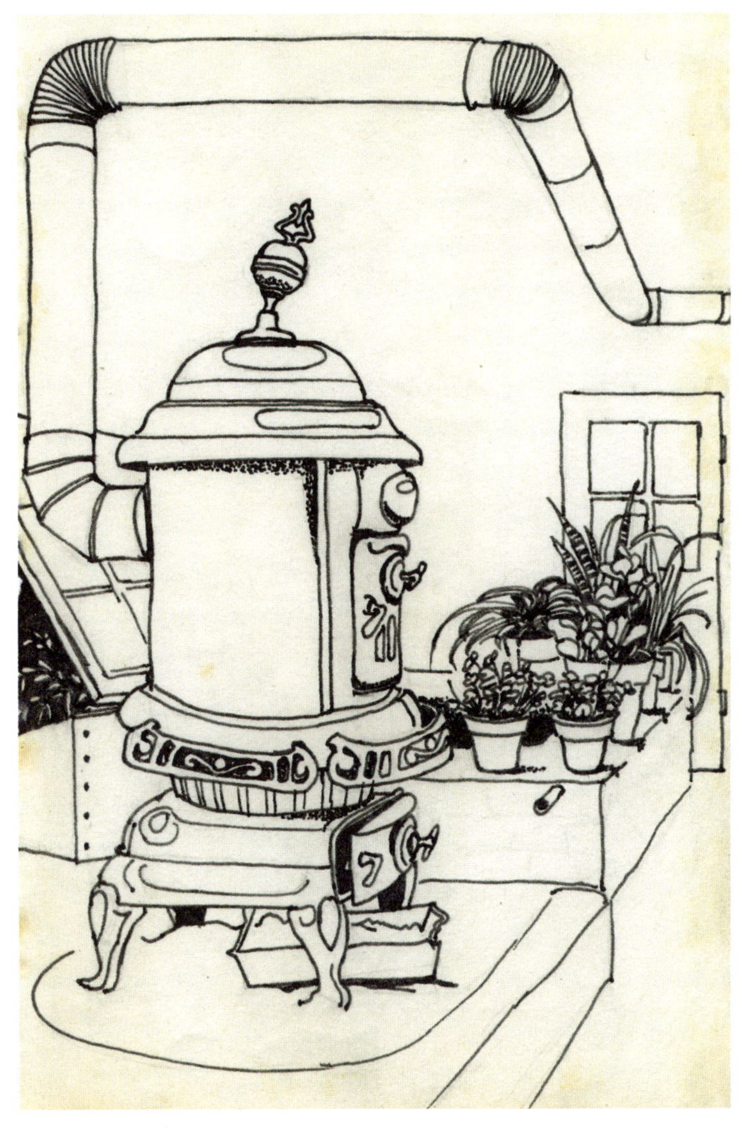

Stove and Pipe, 1956
Pen and ink on paper, 21.3 x 13.7cm

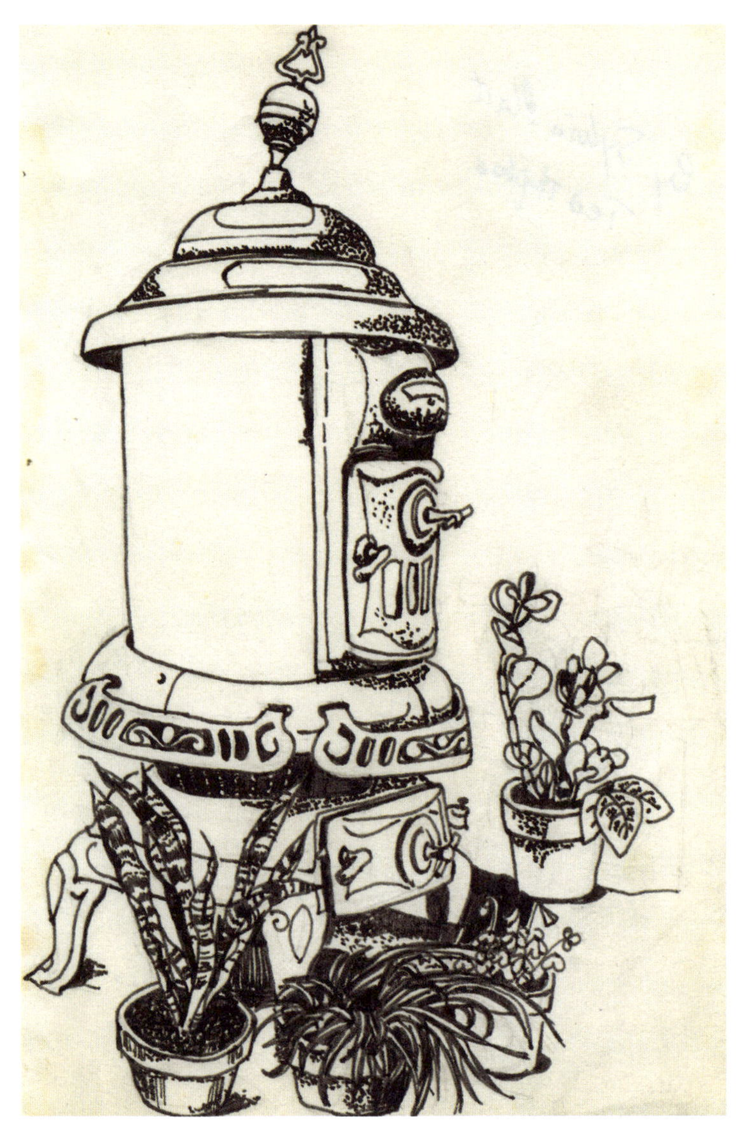

Stove, 1956
Pen and ink on paper, 21.3 x 13.7cm

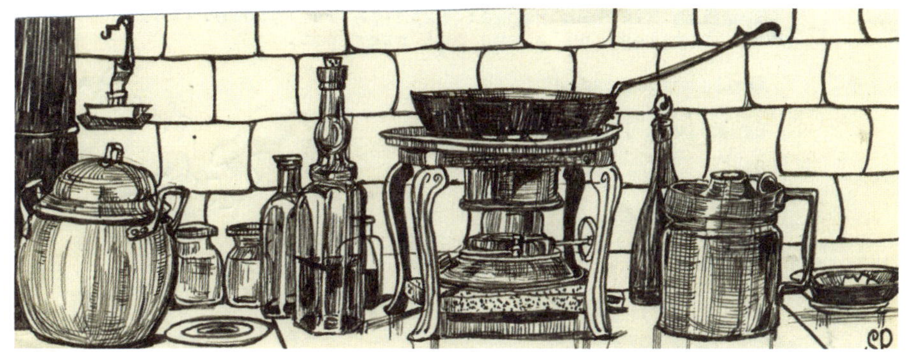

Spanish Kitchen Range: with Petrol Stove, Oil Bottles, Milk Can and Stew Pot, 1956
Pen and ink on paper, 6.5 x 16.8cm

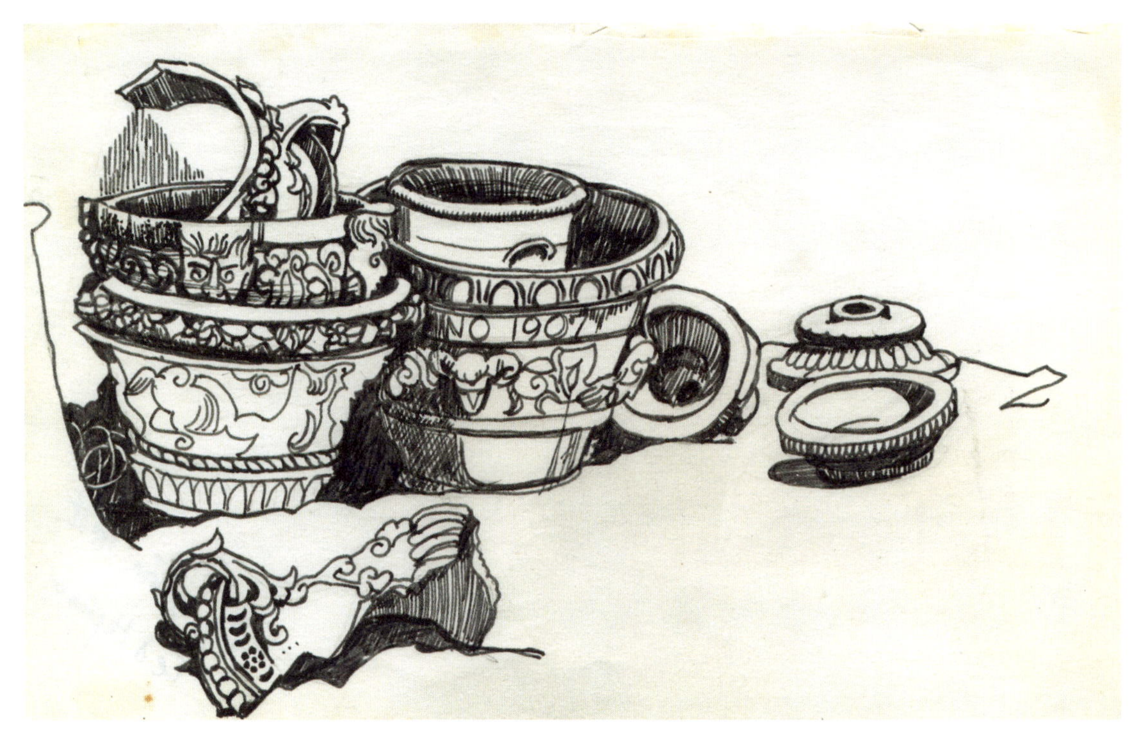

Pots, 1956
Pen and ink on paper, 14 x 21cm

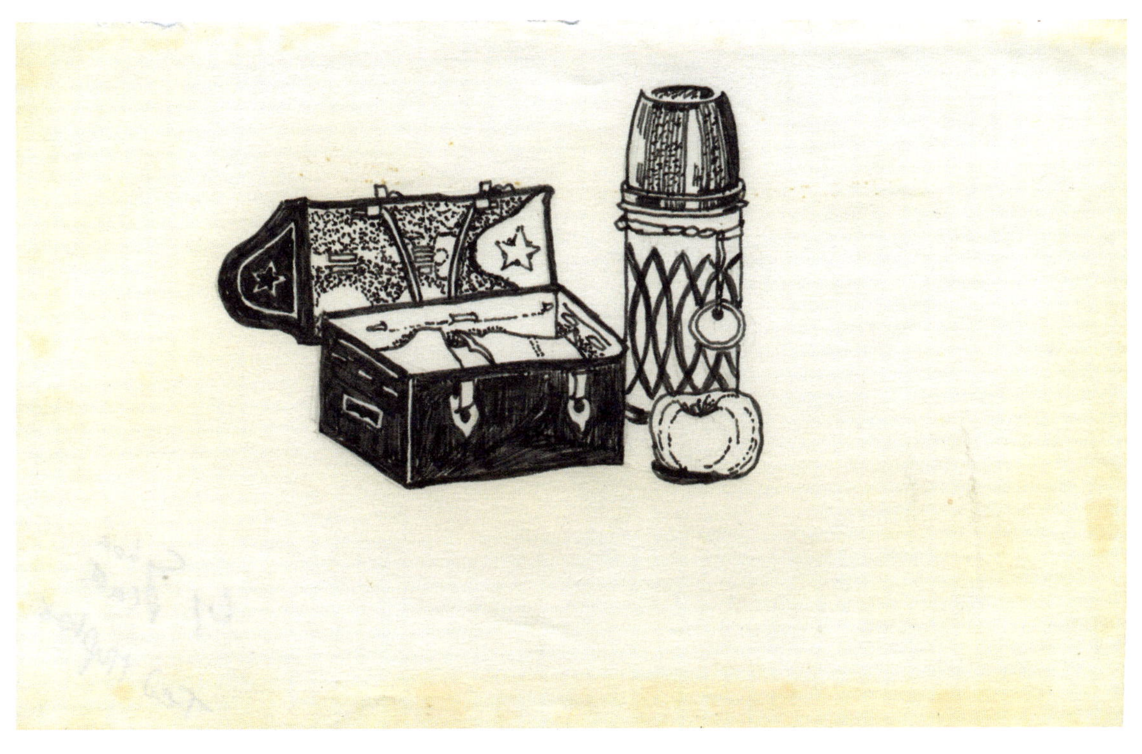

Box and Flask, 1956
Pen and ink on paper, 13.4 x 21cm

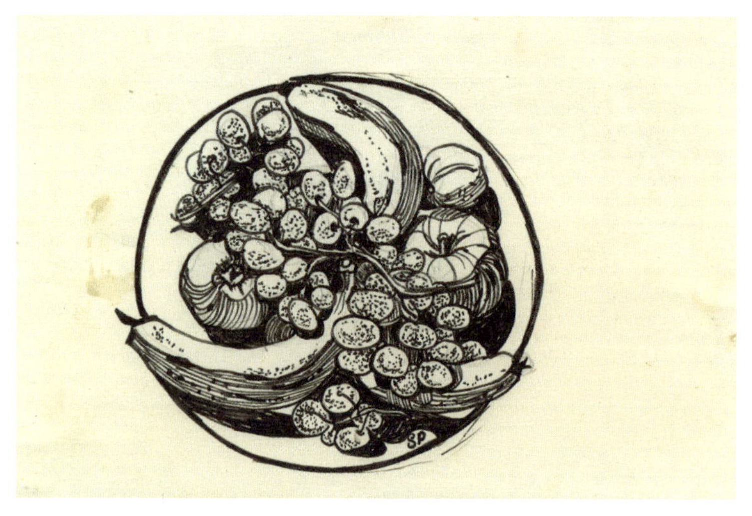

Bowl of Fruit, 1956
Pen and ink on paper, 9.8 x 14cm

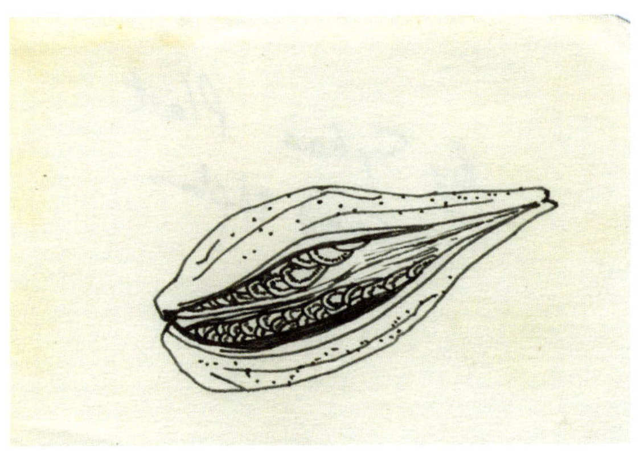

Pod, 1956
Pen and ink on paper, 7.3 x 10.5cm

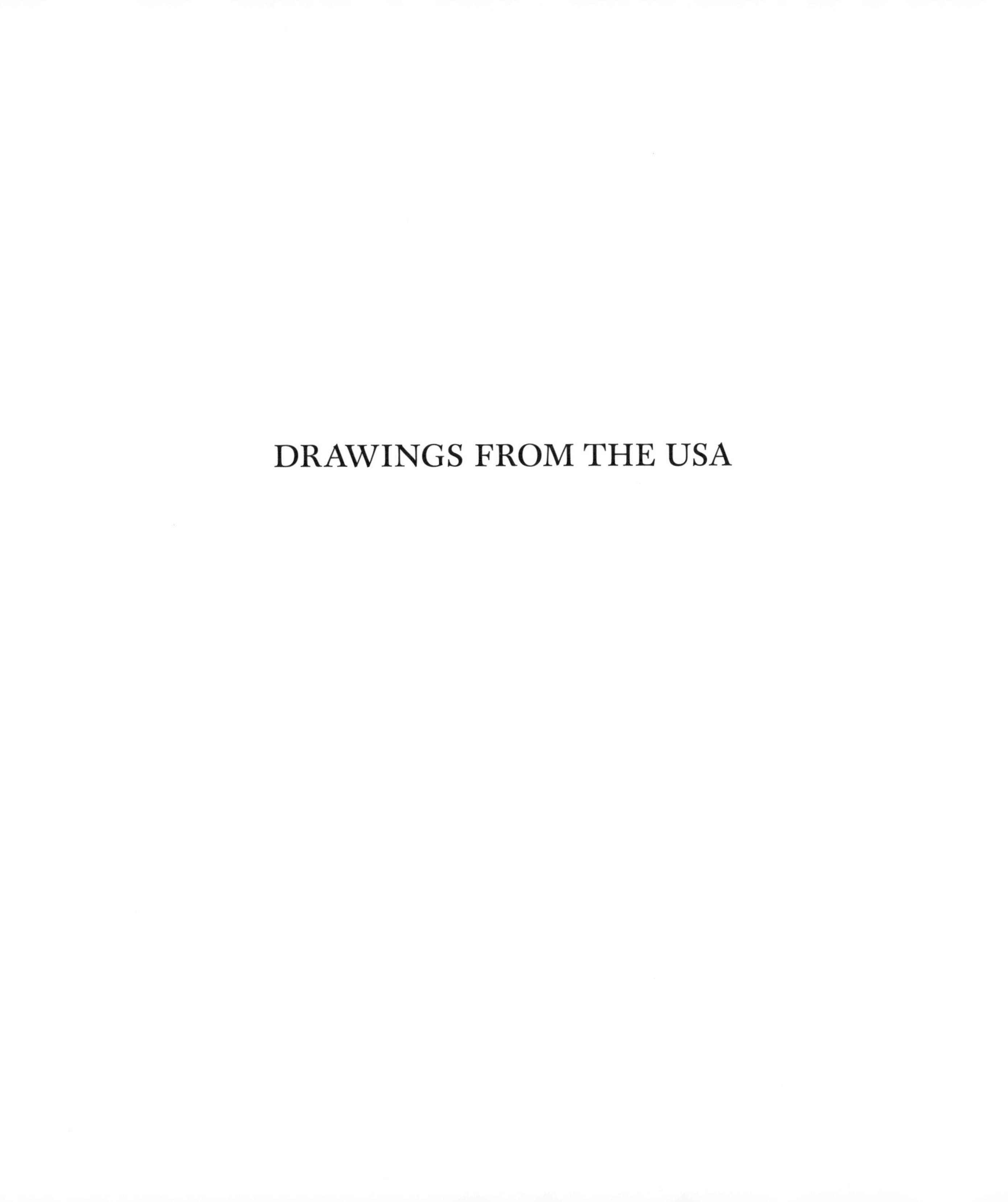

DRAWINGS FROM THE USA

Wednesday: August 21, 1957

A low, sultry day. The sky a luminous white glower of light. I am caught in the six days before this is over. Stops and starts. In love with Henry James: Beast in the jungle robs me of fear of job because of love of story, always trying to present it in mind, as to a class. The first week will be the worst, but from Sept. 1st on, I'll outline my first four weeks & prepare them in detail & become familiar with the library again. So there. Once I get into the blissful concreteness of this job, my life will catapult into a new phase: that I know. Experience, various students, specific problems. The blessed edges and rounds of the real, the factual.

Every day to jot down notes: a husband uses the birthday card from his mother-in-law as a penwiper. Whole relationship jumps into focus. Kindly unadmired unloved mother-in-law. Problem of aging parents.

Yesterday: the weird spectacle of fiddler crabs in the mud-pools off Rock Harbor creek: a mud flat at low tide, surrounded by a margin of dried brittle marsh grass, stretching away into the yellow-green salt marsh. Mud, damp toward center, alive with the rustle and carapaced scuttle of green-black fiddler crabs, like an evil cross between spiders and lobsters and crickets, bearing one gigantic pale green claw and walking sideways. At our approaching footsteps, the crabs near the bank scuttled up it, into holes in the black mucky earth, and into the grass roots, and the crabs in the soggy black center of the dried pool dug themselves into the mud, under little mud lids until only claws jutted from the little cliff of the bank, and elbows and eyes looked out of the myriad holes among the roots of the dry grasses and the drying clustered musselshells, like some crustaceous bulbs among the tussocks. An image: weird, of another world, with its own queer habits, of mud, lumped, under-peopled with quiet crabs.

A light vivid Harper's article on Cambridge. A couple of short colorful articles on Eastham to go with drawings of Mrs. Spaulding and beachplums, boats beached in Rock Harbor, and two corn vases.

A story: told with infinite detail, but must <u>move</u>: The corn vases. To balance long sentences, have short fluid sentences. Mrs. McFague, a stolid, goodhearted Cape Codder, indefatigable talker, memory runs back to Frisco quake, thrown together with young couple in her cottages without car, takes them shopping, to doctor's. Sense of her simplicity, yet she hides riches: antiques: two corn vases in trailer, amid poverty. Lazy, unimaginative, sickly husband: get in story of second marriage through present talk: husband with abscessed ear: visitors descend on them: Mrs. McFague's lack of willpower, contrast with Tookie, who would consider such an invasion outrageous. Mrs. McFague comes back to find children playing with corn vases, utter weakminded wills of parents. Main theme: parental weakness. Mrs. McFague sends them off. Tookie, no children, English husband.

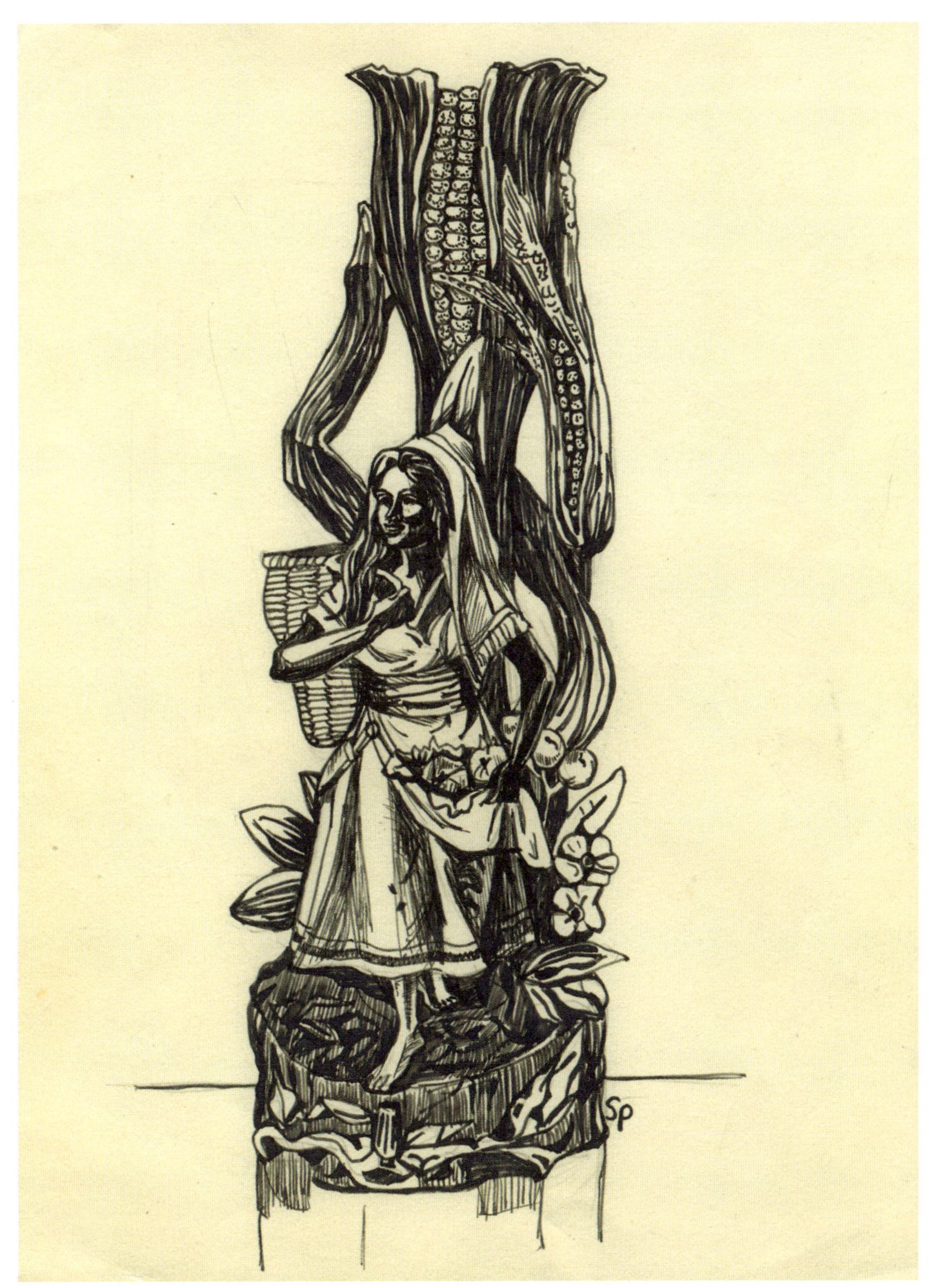

Study of Corn Vase, 1957
Pen and ink on paper, 25.5 x 17.8cm

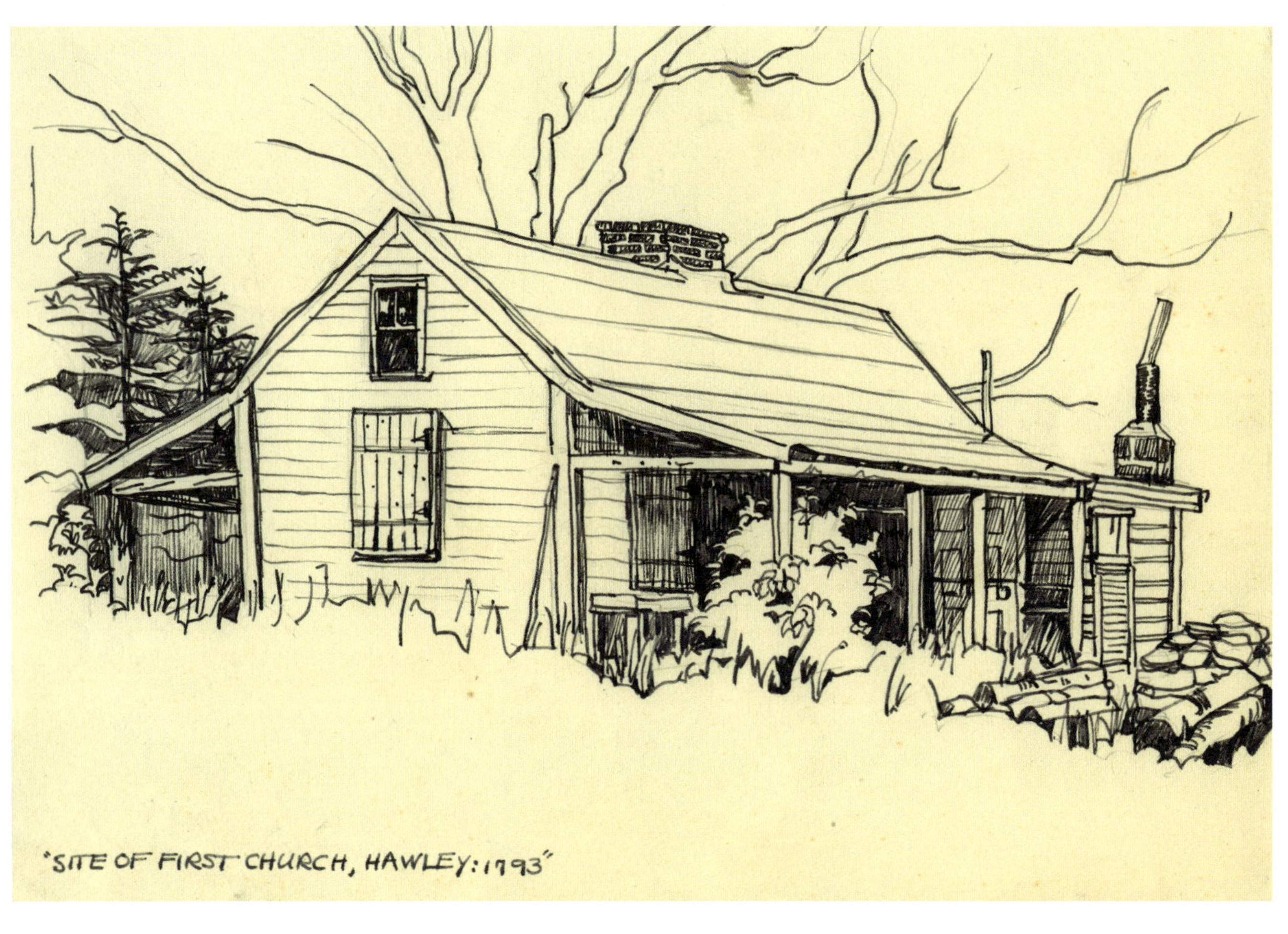

Site of First Church, Hawley, 1793, 1957
Pencil, pen and ink on paper, 17.8 x 25.5cm

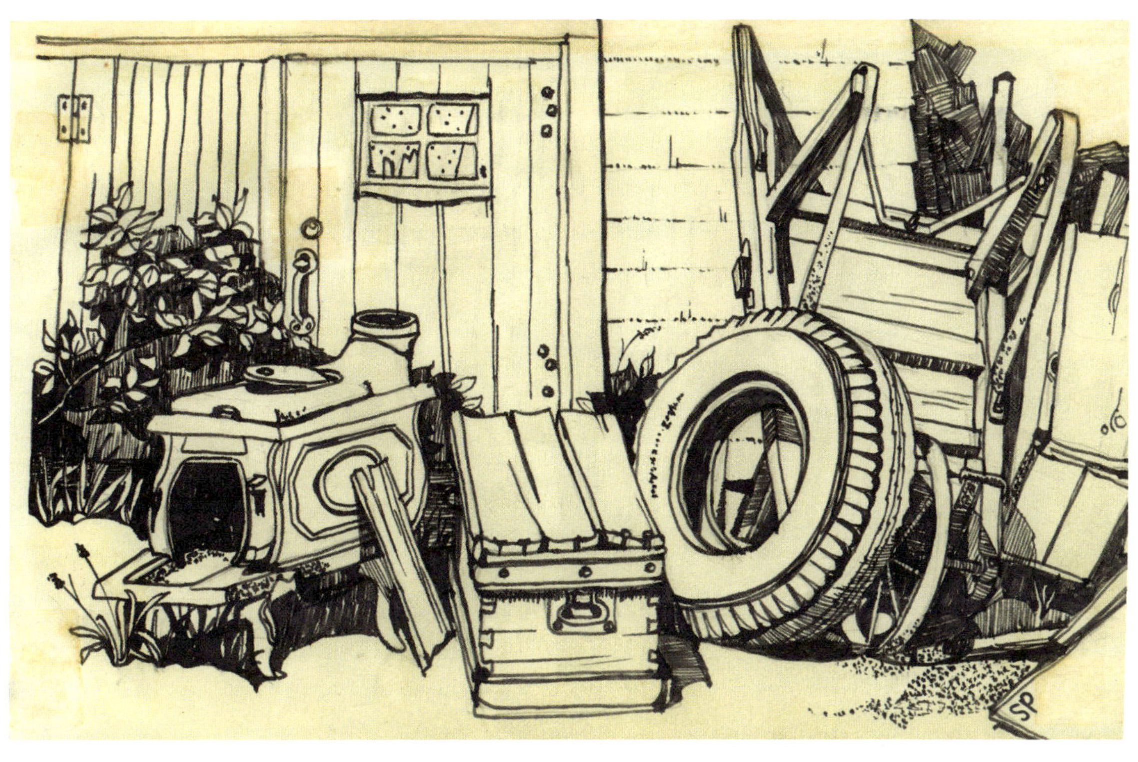

The Pleasure of Odds and Ends, 1957
Pen and ink on paper, 14 x 21.5cm

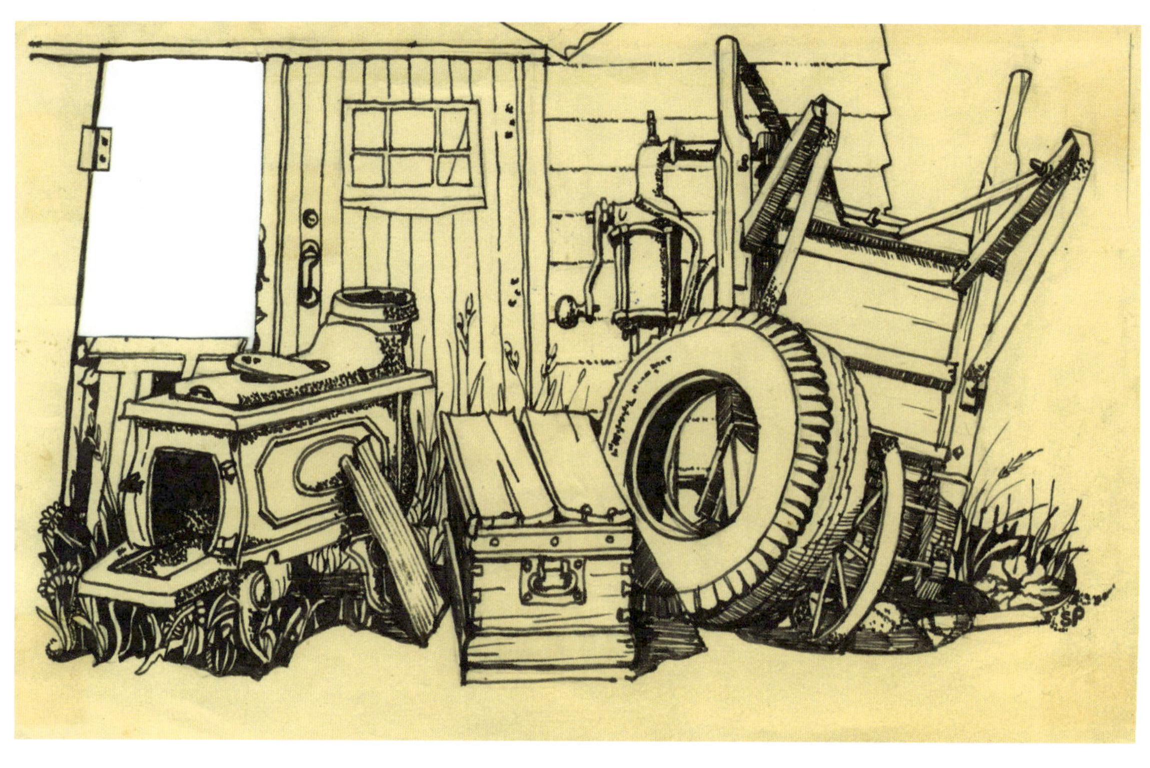

The Pleasure of Odds and Ends 2, 1957
Pen and ink on paper, 14 x 21.5cm

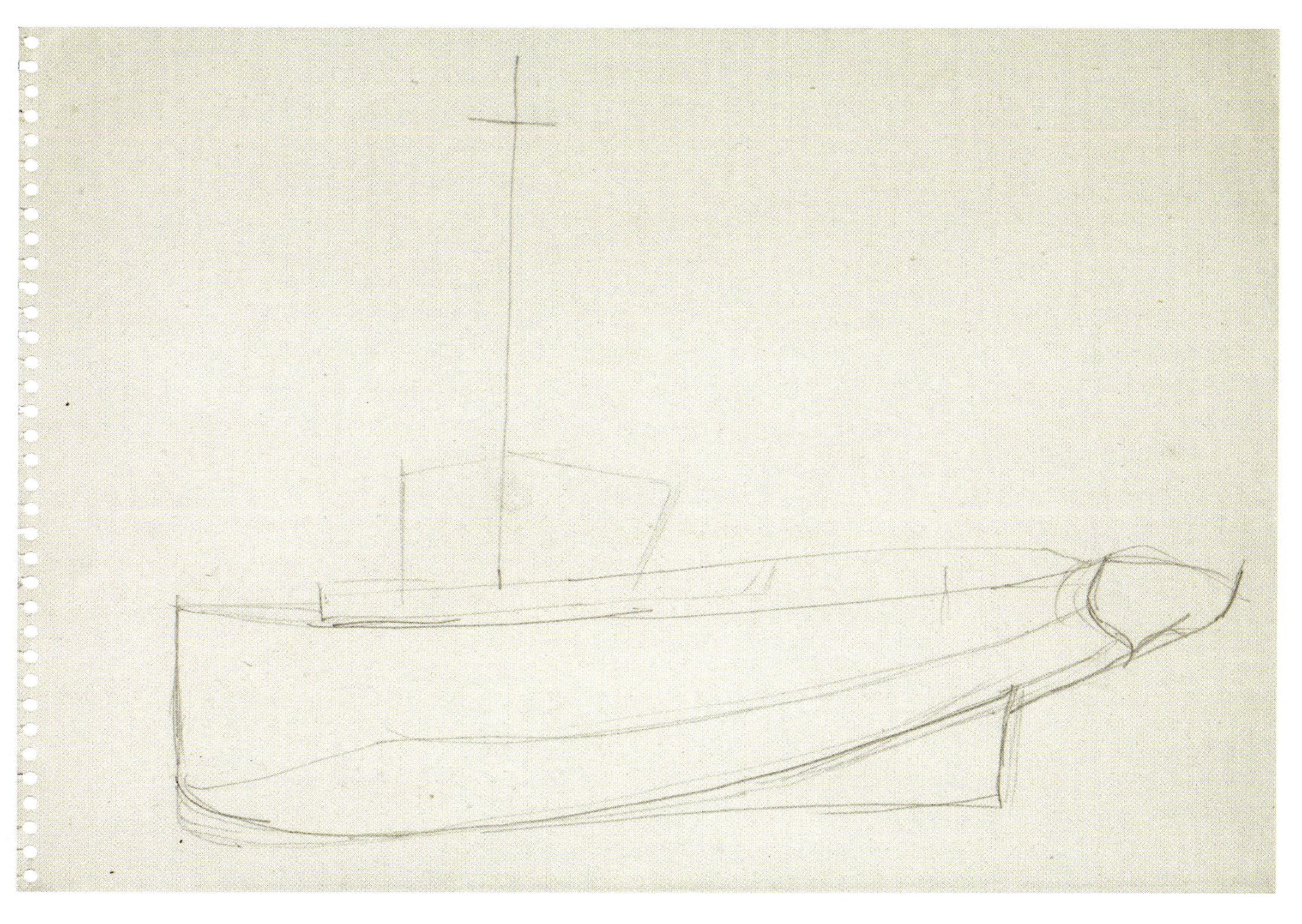

Sketch for a Boat, 1956
Pencil on paper, 17.8 x 25.5cm

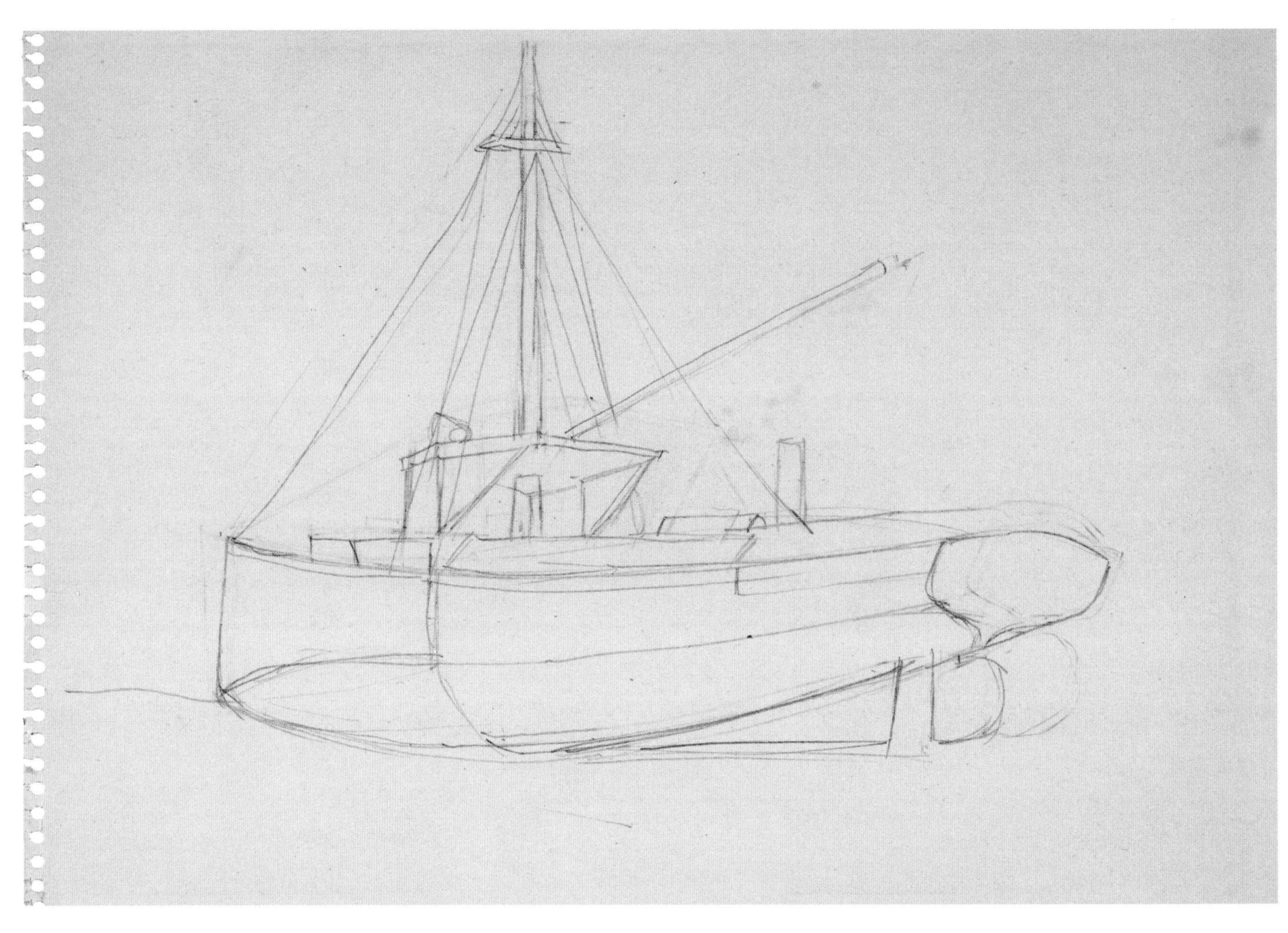

Study of a Boat, 1956
Pencil on paper, 17.8 x 25.5cm

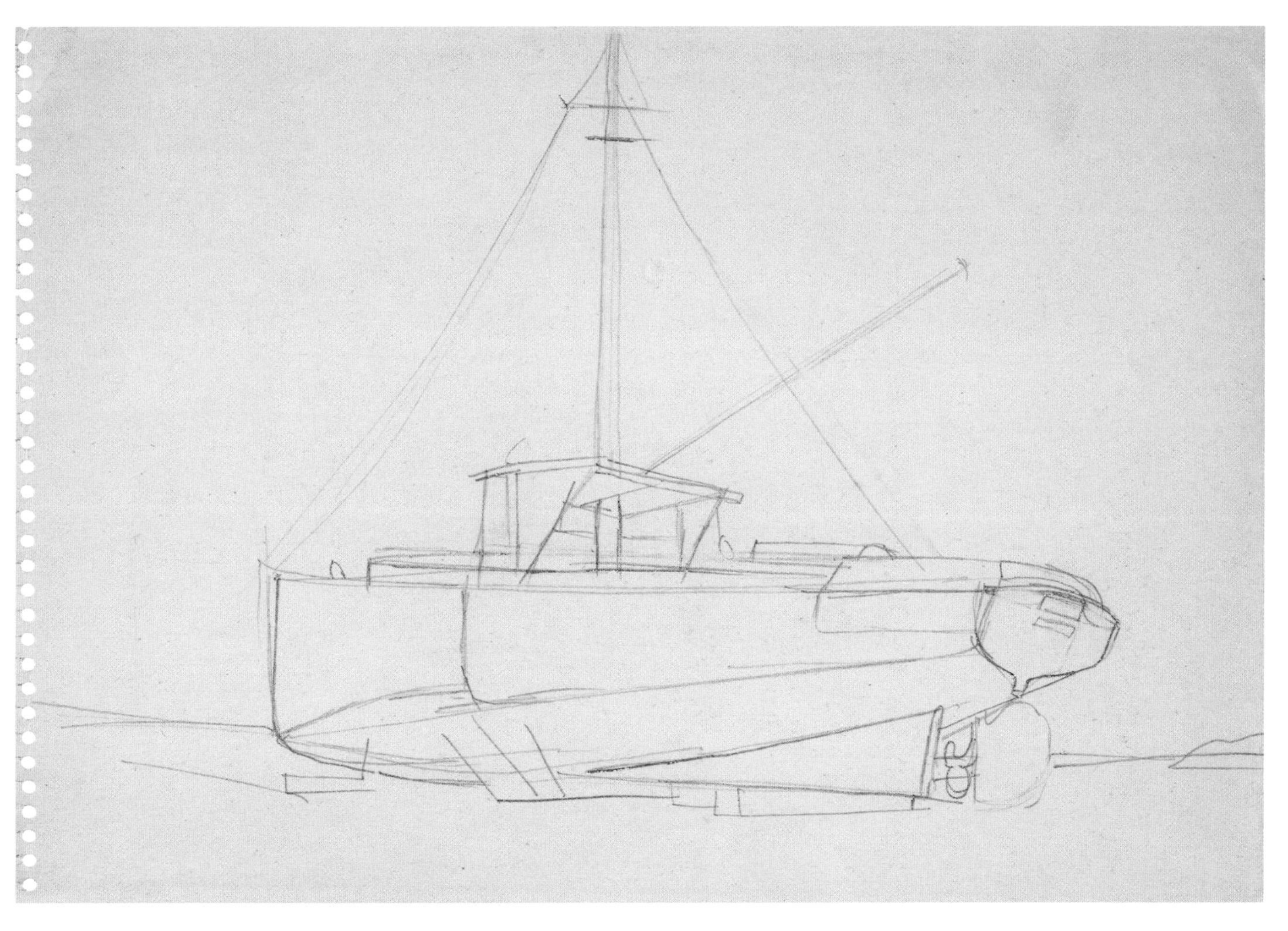

Study of a Fishing Boat, 1956
Pencil on paper, 17.8 x 25.5cm

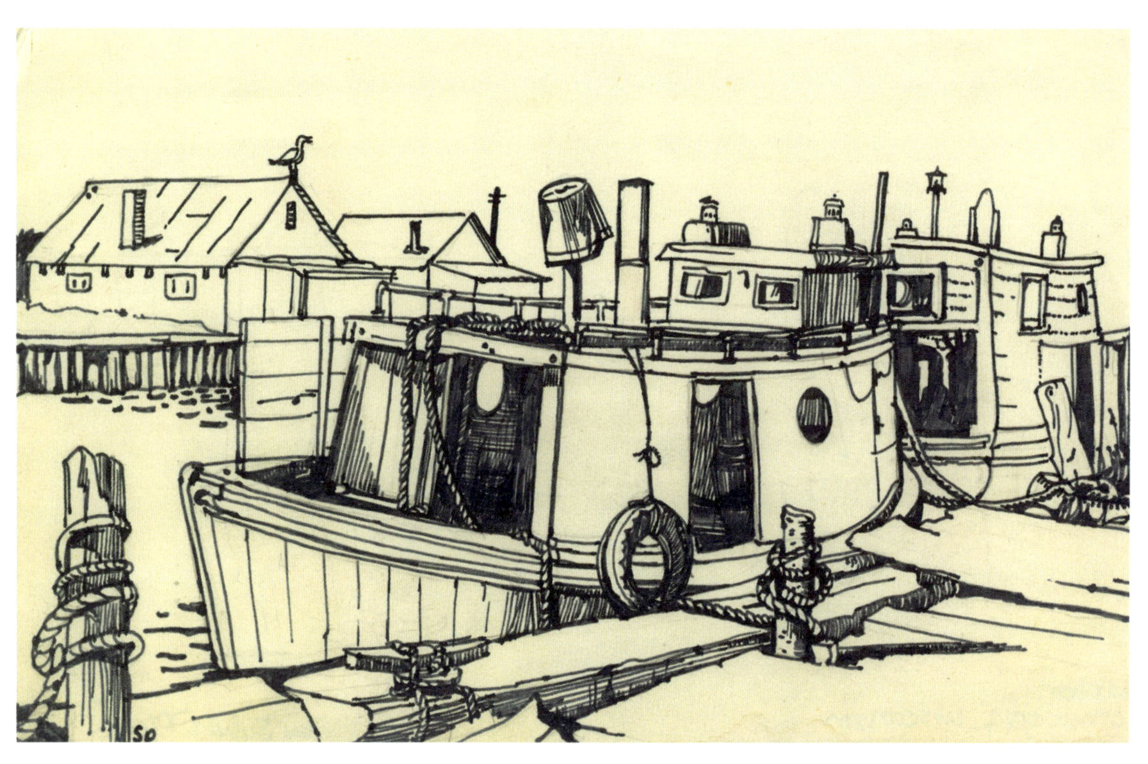

Harbour Cornucopia, Wisconsin
Pen and ink on paper, 14 x 21.3cm

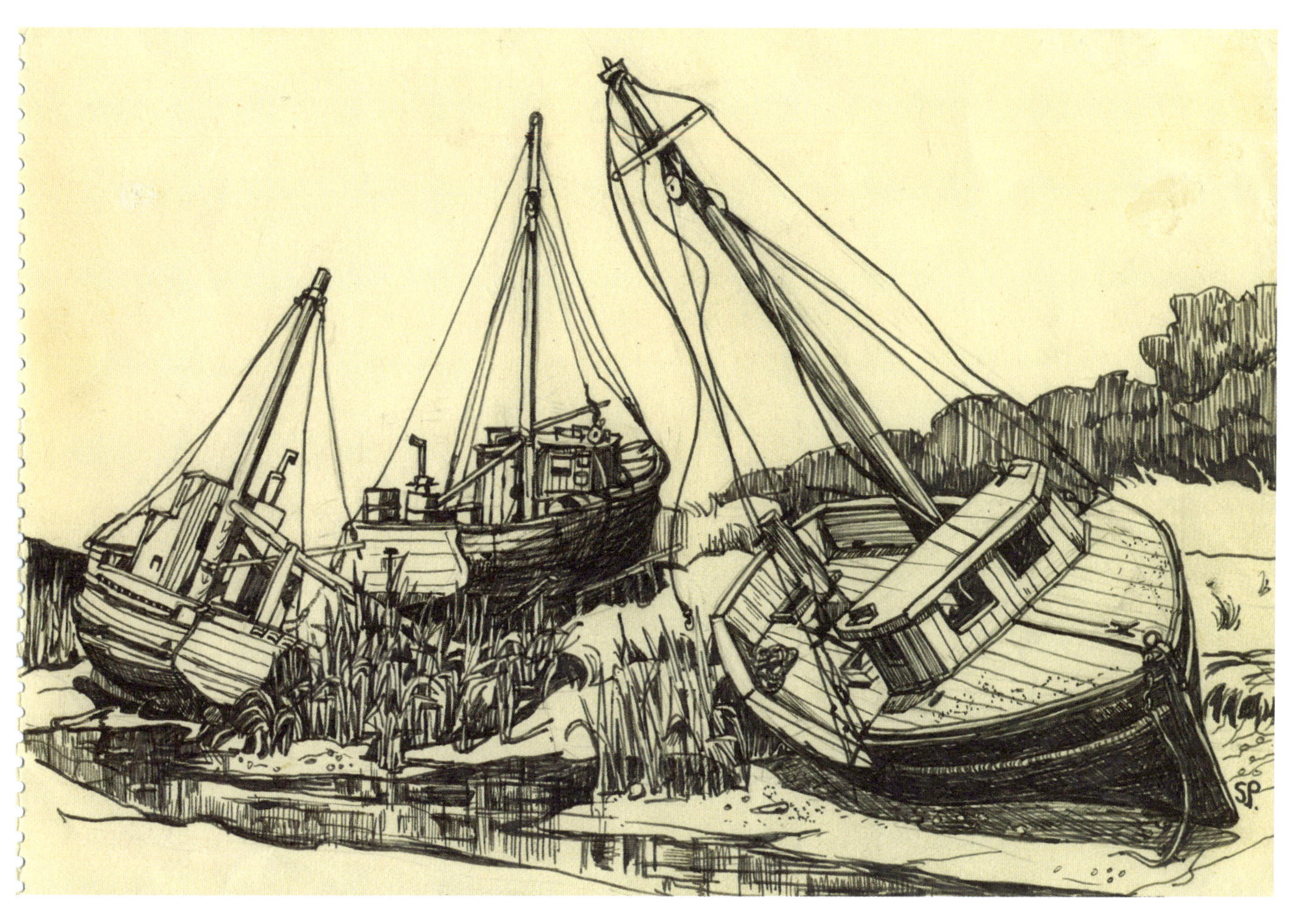

Boat off Rock Harbour, Cape Cod
Pen and ink on paper, 17.8 x 25.5cm

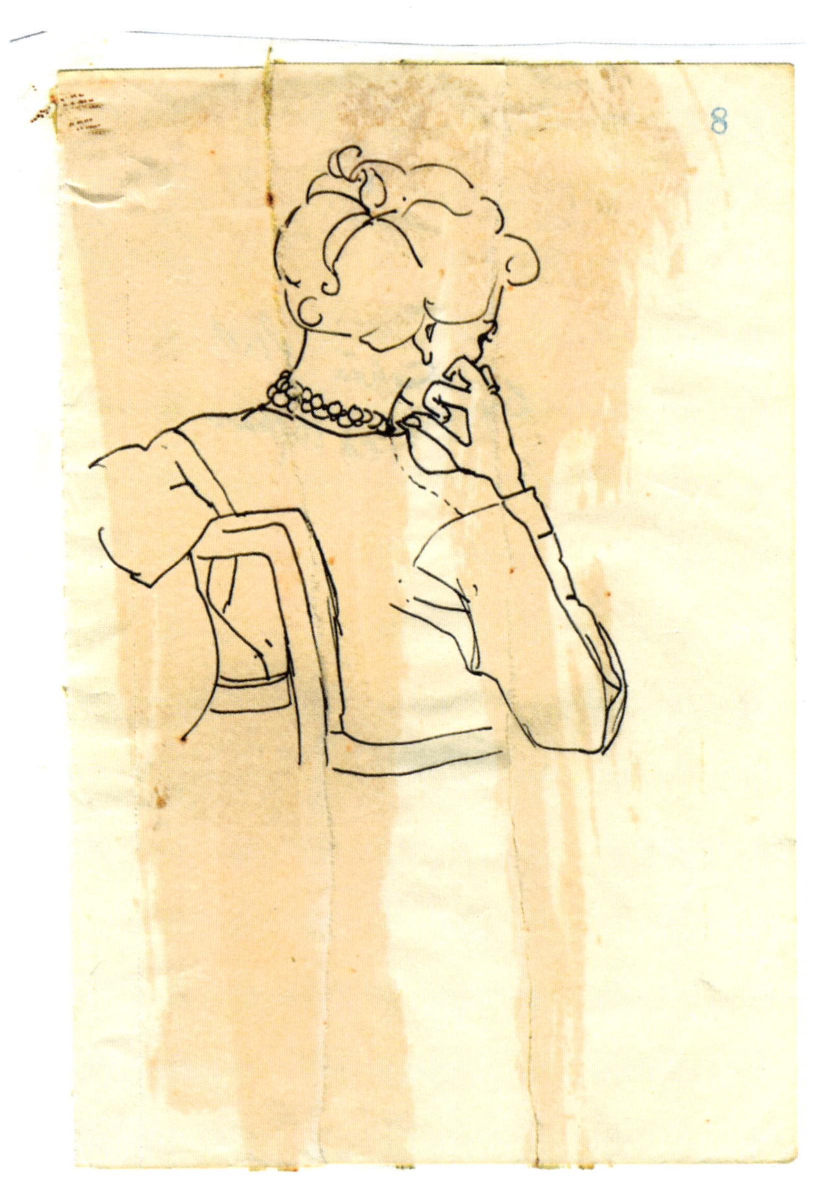

Study of a Seated Figure, c. 1957
Pen and ink on paper, 21 x 14cm

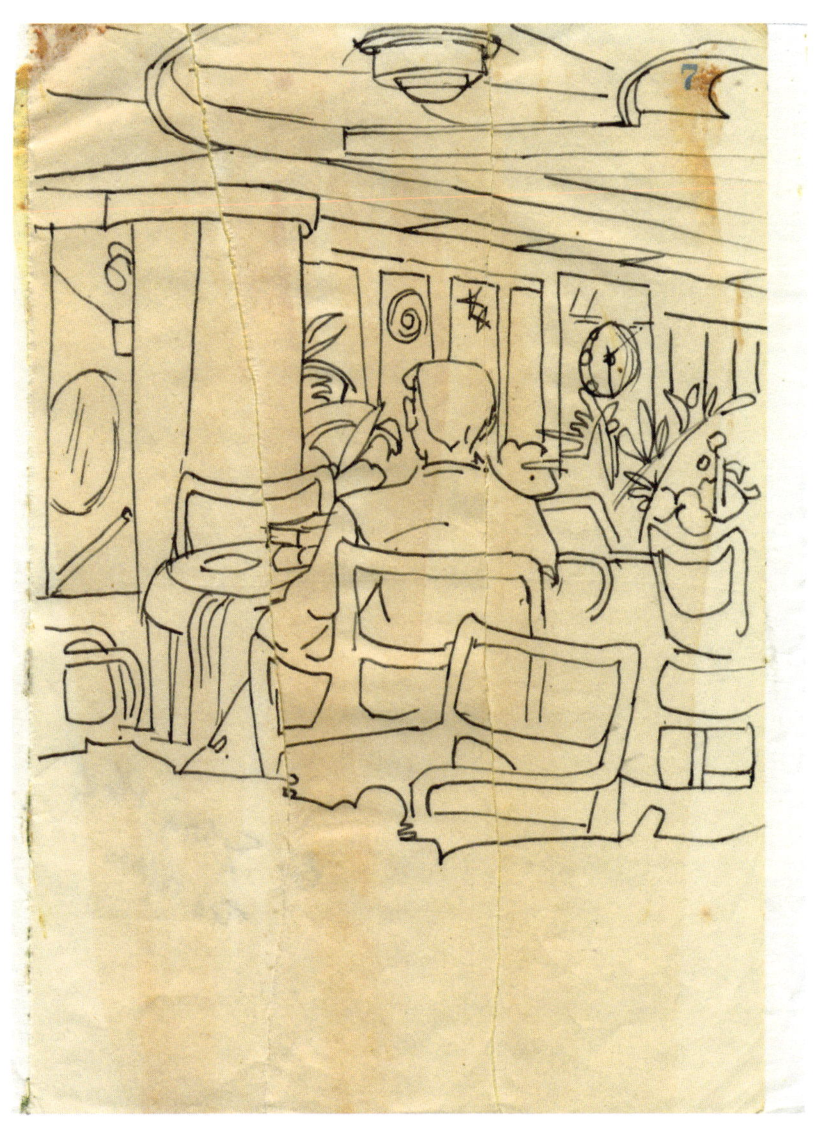

Sketch of Restaurant Interior, c. 1957
Pen and ink on paper, 21 x 13.7cm

BIOGRAPHY

Sylvia Plath born on 27 October 1932 at 2.10pm in the Massachusetts Memorial Hospital in Boston, USA.

1935, 27 April: Sylvia's brother, Warren, born.

1936, Autumn: Plath's family moved from 24 Prince Street, Jamaica Plain to 92 Johnson Avenue, Winthrop, Massachusetts.

1940, 5 November: Plath's father, Otto Plath, died following an amputation of his leg, which was a result of unattended diabetes.

1942, October: Plath's mother, Aurelia, and her brother, Warren, moved to 26 Elmwood Road, Wellesley, Mass.

1950: Sylvia Plath attended Smith College

1953: Suicide attempt with sleeping pills on 24 August. Missed the autumn term at Smith College.

1954: Attended Harvard summer school.

1955, 6 June: graduated from Smith College.

1955, October to 1957, June: Attended Newnham College at Cambridge University, reading English on a Fulbright fellowship from the States.

1956, 16 June: Married Ted Hughes in the Church of St George the Martyr, Queen Square, London, and honeymooned in France and Spain, June to August.

1956: Plath and Hughes moved to a flat in 55 Eltisley Avenue, Cambridge.

1957, June: Plath completed her BA degree at Cambridge University.

1957, 25 June: Plath and Hughes arrived in New York having crossed the Atlantic on the *Queen Elizabeth II*.

1957: They spent the summer at Cape Cod before moving to an apartment at 337 Elm Street, Northampton, Mass. Plath was an instructor of freshman English at Smith College 1957–58. Hughes was an instructor of English Literature and Creative Writing at the Amherst campus of the University of Massachusetts, 1958.

1958, July: A group of poems written around this time, including 'Lorelei' and 'Full Fathom Five', coincided with Plath's decision to leave teaching and begin writing in earnest.

1958, September: The couple moved to an apartment at 9 Willow Street, Boston. Plath worked as a part-time secretary at the Massachusetts General Hospital's adult psychiatric clinic.

1959: Plath worked part-time for the chairman of the department of Sanskrit and Indian studies at Harvard University, audited Robert Lowell's poetry-writing course at Boston University and was undergoing therapy with Dr Ruth Beuscher. In June Plath fell pregnant.

1959, 9 September to 19 November: Plath and Hughes were guests at Yaddo, an artist's colony in Saratoga Springs, New York, where Sylvia completed the poems which were to become *The Colossus*. They moved back to the UK in December to live in a flat at 3 Chalcot Square, Primrose Hill, London.

1959: Plath wrote 'The Stones', one of the last poems she would write in the States. Later, Plath would see this poem as the dividing line between her juvenilia and her later poems.

1960, 1 April: Frieda Hughes born at Chalcot Square.

1960, 31 October: *The Colossus and Other Poems* published by William Heinemann, Ltd.

1961, March: Sylvia wrote 'Tulips', which would go on to appear in *Ariel*. Hughes noted that this marked a change in her writing practice, observing the speed of her writing increased.

1961, 30 August: Ted Hughes, Sylvia Plath and Frieda
    Hughes moved to Court Green, their new home in
    Devon.
1962, 17 January: Nicholas Hughes born at the family
    home in Devon.
1962, April: Sylvia wrote a number of poems, including
    'Elm', which would be amongst those collected in *Ariel*.
1962, October: Ted and Sylvia separated.
1962, October–November: Almost all the poems in *Ariel*
    were written in these two months, often two or three
    each day, including 'Daddy' on 12 October.
1962, 10 December: Plath closed up the Devonshire house
    and moved to 23 Fitzroy Road, London.
1963, 14 January: *The Bell Jar* was published, under the
    pseudonym Victoria Lucas, by William Heinemann,
    Ltd.
1963, February: Six poems – 'Balloons', 'Kindness', 'Edge',
    'Contusion', 'Words' and 'Mystic' – were written during
    the last ten days of Sylvia's life.
1963, 11 February: Sylvia Plath committed suicide at 23
    Fitzroy Road.
1965: *Ariel* published by Faber and Faber, edited and
    arranged by Ted Hughes.
1966: *The Bell Jar* published by Faber and Faber under
    Sylvia Plath's name.
1971: Two volumes of Plath's poetry, *Crossing the Water* and
    Winter Trees, published by Faber and Faber.
1981: *Collected Poems* appeared, followed by *Selected Poems*
    two years later, both published by Faber and Faber.

BIBLIOGRAPHY

POETRY
The Colossus
Ariel
Crossing the Water
Winter Trees
Collected Poems
Selected Poems
Ariel: The Restored Edition

PROSE
The Bell Jar
Johnny Panic and the Bible of Dreams
Mary Ventura and the Ninth Kingdom

FOR CHILDREN
The Bed Book
The It-Doesn't-Matter Suit
Collected Children's Stories

NON-FICTION
Letters Home: Correspondence 1950–1963
edited by Aurelia Schober Plath
The Journals of Sylvia Plath 1950–1962
edited by Karen V. Kukil
The Letters of Sylvia Plath: Volumes I and II
edited by Peter K. Steinberg and Karen V. Kukil